Philadelphia
Reflections

Philadelphia Reflections

Stories from the Delaware to the Schuylkill

Edited by

COLLEEN LUTZ CLEMENS &
REBECCA HELM BEARDSALL

Charleston   London

THE
History
PRESS

Published by The History Press
Charleston, SC 29403
www.historypress.net

Images are courtesy of the authors unless otherwise noted.

Cover images: Security Elavator Company, 1942. *Courtesy of Heather Goodman*; Philadelphia skyline. *Conrad Erb.*

First published 2011

Manufactured in the United States

ISBN 978.1.60949.318.9

Library of Congress Cataloging-in-Publication Data

Philadelphia reflections : stories from the Delaware to the Schuylkill / edited by Colleen Clemens and Rebecca Beardsall.
p. cm.
ISBN 978-1-60949-318-9
1. Philadelphia (Pa.)--History--Anecdotes. 2. Philadelphia Region (Pa.)--History, Local--Anecdotes. 3. Lehigh River Valley (Pa.)--History, Local--Anecdotes. 4. Philadelphia (Pa.)--Biography--Anecdotes. 5. Philadelphia Region (Pa.)--History--Anecdotes. 6. Philadelphia (Pa.)--Social life and customs--Anecdotes. 7. Philadelphia Region (Pa.)--Social life and customs--Anecdotes. I. Clemens, Colleen. II. Beardsall, Rebecca.
F158.36.P45 2011
974.8'11--dc23
2011031268

Notice: The information in this book is true and complete to the best of our knowledge. It is offered without guarantee on the part of the authors or The History Press. The authors and The History Press disclaim all liability in connection with the use of this book.

For Dwayne and Weasel

Contents

Acknowledgements

We are both thankful for our Pennsylvania heritage and for our parents—Robert and Marilyn Helm and Sandra and Barry Lutz—for raising us in the tradition of the Pennsylvania German community, which cultivated our work ethic and love of Pennsylvania.

We appreciate the honesty, patience and talent evident in all of the writers who generously shared their memories and stories of Pennsylvania. Reflecting on the past is never an easy task, and we are grateful that they were willing to take that journey with us.

Finally, we would like to thank our partners, Matthew Clemens and Geoffrey Beardsall, for listening to book talk over many a Sunday breakfast. Without your relentless support, this book would not exist.

Introduction

Almost thirteen million people live in Pennsylvania as of 2010. They spread out over forty-six thousand square miles. Some of them live in the middle of the state in Happy Valley, where they can hear cheers celebrating a Nittany Lions touchdown from a mile away. Others fall asleep to the sounds of peepers that serenade Bucks County residents in the spring. In the fall, neighbors in Hazleton hear children jumping into piled crisp leaves. And in the winter, residents of Erie might hear nothing but the swoosh of snow falling.

Pennsylvania is not only the Keystone State, which was crucial in the founding of this nation, but it is also the keystone to the lives of Pennsylvanians. It is our relationship with the towns, cities and farmland of Pennsylvania that grounds us and provides the support for our livelihoods. Our lives have been shaped by the values, cultures and traditions established in this great state. Coming to an understanding of our sense of place is important to how we view ourselves. This collection of creative nonfiction about the land, people, towns and cities of Pennsylvania was created for us to remember our history and heritage and to honor our present-day lives and accomplishments. The state represents a wide range of individuals; each holds his or her own stories and memories. Even though jobs or families may take Pennsylvanians from their home state, the connection to the place remains.

In 2005, along with two other Pennsylvania writers, we presented creative nonfiction essays focusing on the land of Pennsylvania at a conference. We realized our panel could be the beginning of a larger collection that would present readers with a full view of Pennsylvania's regions through the eyes of some of the state's best nonfiction essay writers. As two lifetime residents of Pennsylvania, we are proud to have edited two works that reflect the beauty, work ethic and tradition we see in the Keystone State: *Philadelphia Reflections: Stories from the Delaware to the Schuylkill* and *Western Pennsylvania Reflections: Stories from the Alleghenies to Lake Erie.*

We wanted to hear the stories from these thousands of square miles, the stories that come up from out of the ground of the mines and from the mills, from the stadiums and the stables, from the fire halls and the fishing holes. We invite you to share in stories from the state, to linger in the spaces you find comfortable and to learn something new about your neighbors who live on a different square mile. Let this book serve as a keystone that holds all of us—residents and transplants alike—together.

No 13 on the B Line

Allentown

By Colleen Lutz Clemens

My family played bingo for money and for meat. On school nights, my mother's side of the family—the Adams side—went to Johnny's bingo hall in Allentown. The wooden floors, veneered with cigarette tar from when players used to be able to smoke inside, groaned from holding up overweight Dutchmen. Though not a lot of kids attended bingo, my sister Stacy and I occupied ourselves. I drew trace sketches of Shirt Tales; Stacy colored. Workers bustled behind the counter getting people their hard bingo cards, two grids per board. "Edelweiss" blared from the eight-track system.

Nana sat at the corner seat closest to the caller. She wore a housedress, a grayed zipper down the front. I never saw her wear pants. She was a woman who never wanted to learn how to drive, who drank Coke out of glass bottles and made us pour leftover Froot Loop milk into a Tupperware cup to drink later in the day. She loved bingo. My Adams blood predisposes me to love bingo—and to fall into significant depressions that could hospitalize me like my mother and sister, to scratch holes in my head like Nana or even lead to my death like my aunt Donna, whom we called Auntie Weasel thanks to *Never Tease A Weasel*, a children's book she gave me.

Nana watched the caller to know the number before it was announced. The numbers bounced like movie popcorn. If the balls arose at the perfect angle, Nana knew she was about to win. The family nudged each other and whispered, "We're open" when she needed one last number. With a win, Nana's arm came up from her sleeveless housecoat, her skin folded, her triceps wiggling without self-awareness. Concentric circles of skin lined her elbows. The moment of winning took away Nana's worries over one daughter so ill she would die at thirty-eight, a disabled grandson, an alcoholic husband and a second daughter who towed the line of sadness more often than not. A bingo meant pocket money for the next walk to the Liberty Lunch with her smart-assed, know-it-all granddaughter who needed to be fed before she got gretzy.

When Mom or Nana called bingo, everyone else in the hall groaned, many of them open for the four corners, the postage stamp or the upside-down T. They awaited a different number to give them the jolt of a win. Smiles of congratulations tinged with jealousy and grumbling came from the table's other end. Nana and Mom often did well—today my mother's license plate reads "LUCKIEE." The coverall—where one gets every space on the board—was worth the big bucks. Even in the 1980s, these games were worth over $1,000. When Nana won this game, we felt the relief and the urgency in her bingo call. Our ears waited to hear if someone else in the rest of the hall called out at the same time, like two birds laying claim to the same nest. If no one cuckolded her win, tears started in the corners of her eyes behind her plastic glasses. When she saw the number before it was called, she knew for a second before anyone else that in one more beat everything about life would be just a little bit better. The Adams clan didn't hear the groans. All we heard was Nana, panting, out of breath, talking to her daughters as the checker called one number at a time to ensure the win's validity. No one in our family ever made a bingo mistake.

<hr />

When I was eight, I started to work as a board girl. Wearing polyester shorts and coiled plastic bracelets, I walked the hall so disgruntled players could exchange boards that weren't winning that night. The heavy stacks of hard boards nestled into my right elbow. I usually had a boy's initials written onto the top of my hand, a KK for Kevin, whose family would sue mine in a few years, or an NR for Nicky, who would die in a car accident after graduation. Picky players demanded boards to match their superstitions: no 13 in the B column, O-69 in the corner, no 40s in the N column. With one hand, I clicked one board after another, a muted cardboard *thwap!* as each board hit the one below it. The boards' corners were soft and fibery. Kind players remembered my efforts and slipped me a quarter or even a dollar after a big win. Sometimes they kissed me on the cheek if they won the coverall. Men seemed to do that more often than women.

But local ordinances prohibited Allentonians from gambling for money on Sundays, so we found a bingo game with prizes—not money, but meat—in Topton. Stacy and I fought over who got to sit seatbelt-less in the front seat of the brown Monte Carlo. Mennonites in horses and buggies slowed traffic on the one-lane highway. Auntie Weasel and my cousin John came, along with Nana and Pappy. John, a product of thalidomide, used his half arms to circle vowels in Sears and JC Penney's catalogues, while the rest of us marked our boards. Postage stamp for a T-bone, four corners for pork chops and the big game, the coverall, for a full meal, including a roast, potatoes and corn, if it was in season. Folding tables lined the fire hall. Our family filled a table in the center of the hall every Sunday. No money at stake, just food. But Stacy and I loved the Sunday games because we got to play, unlike at Johnny's, where laws disallowed ten-year-olds from gambling. Stacy and I got our own boards and dabbers. We lined the table with our own good luck charms—mine a plastic blue Smurfette and a yellow-haired troll doll. To pass the time, I chanted mantras in my head. One day, I won a pack of chicken while humming the lines of a Stayfree commercial. I believed this song enchanted me and sang it to myself for the next three hours. When we won, everyone cheered for us.

If more than one player called bingo, no one got the meat. I *hoped* there would be another winner, though I would never make such an admission to my family. Instead, the simultaneous winners got Dutch butter cookies in a white cardboard box with cerulean letters, a hex sign drawn on the side. While a disappointment to Nana, Mom and Weasel, the cookies, all yellowy and topped with sugar sprinkles in pink or green, were a big win to a kid. I loved that the family could eat them right at the table, instead of just getting a ticket redeemable for a hunk of meat.

Auntie Weasel and Mom were the loudest women in the hall. Those games must have been a relief from my aunt's life in a trailer park, dimmed with poverty and depression. Often, her fridge only had a jar of pickles and a two-foot block of fluorescent government cheese. One Sunday, she started a fire in the trashcan at our table. A chain smoker like so many in my family before her, Weasel threw a still-lit cigarette in the gray plastic bin filled with losing bingo sheets, napkins stained with ketchup and scrap pieces of paper covered with my doodles. She started shrieking. The smoke stopped the game—I saw a game stop only one other time, when a man had a heart attack in the aisle at Johnny's. Stacy, John and I raged with laughter at the commotion. Weasel still had both of her legs then—in another few

Donna ("Weasel") and Sandra Adams (the author's mom) as children.

years, one would be amputated due to gangrene—so she ran around the hall grabbing cans of soda to douse the flames.

On a normal Sunday, during intermission, when everyone else went to get Mars bars and French fries, Pappy took me to the back alley to look for aluminum cans, which he then sold to the scrap man. Before the era of curbside recycling, industrious men and homeless people found they could make a little extra cash from waste left in the streets. When there weren't a lot of cans on the ground, we checked the dumpsters. If cans were in sight, I threw my skinny body over the green edge, avoiding the sticky residue from open bags and food waste. We had a long stick that I used to hook into the little hole for the mouth. Slowly, I raised the stick and rescued the can from the dumpster. Pappy and I called it "fishing." Even though I didn't have a job at meat bingo, I was proud to contribute by slinging my body over the edge of dumpsters. We returned in time to play for chicken breasts and pork chops for the rest of the afternoon.

And then Weasel died. I was at youth group, flirting with the boys on a Sunday night after meat bingo. When I walked in the door, the TV wasn't on, and Mom was in the bathroom crying. My dad told me it was okay to cry, so I hugged the stuffed bear I got that day and sat on the corduroy armchair, crying into the toy's new softness. Weasel was gone. She stood

Lorraine, Charles and a young Sandra.

up, had an aneurysm and died on the trailer's floor in front of John. She was thirty-eight.

I was turning thirteen in four days. Her funeral was on my birthday. Mom called WAEB—the AM radio station the sisters listened to every morning—and Bobby Gunther Walsh said a few words about Weasel over the air. Her fifteen seconds of fame came when she was dead. Nana did her best to make my birthday a happy event, even if it would be marred every year after. Because she had no present for me, she took me to Woolworths at the Whitehall (or the "poor people's") mall. Because she worked there for many years, Nana encountered someone offering condolences around every aisle corner. We walked past the parakeets for sale, the boxed foods and hair ties, and I found myself in the music section. Smitten with River Phoenix in *Stand By Me*, I chose a cassette tape of Oldies music, its metallic liner just as poppy and bright as its music. Nana and I stood at the checkout; she never cried in the store that afternoon. Pappy waited to pick us up outside Leh's department store, where Nana always bought her Jean Naté.

I didn't attend Weasel's funeral. As a new middle schooler, I was sure my friends would continue the tradition of locker decorating for my birthday. Every morning, some girl's locker boasted purple crêpe streamers and pink balloons, even a sign with "Happy Birthday" scribed in bubble letters. The idea of decorations going to waste pressed me to school, even if my troubled, loving aunt was being buried that afternoon. But when I walked down the gray hallway past Mr. Drahuschak's biology classroom, my locker wasn't decorated, and somewhere a few miles away my aunt was being put in the ground. Now Nana and Pappy rest in the same plot, where airplanes fly over their graves.

We stopped believing in God and going to bingo after Weasel died. We couldn't bear to sit with an empty seat at the table. But losing bingo became the least of my family's worries. Mom sank into a depression that required hospitalization. Nana sat in her weathered armchair and played the lottery. She kept spiral notebooks cataloguing every night's winning Daily Number and Big 4 as she looked for patterns in a world that no longer made sense. Jon was dumped at Nana and Pappy's; his stepfather took the family dog instead. Nana started scratching her head, until she had scratched a saucer-sized hole in her skin, the infection reaching her skull. She, too, ended up in the hospital. She never yelled bingo again.

Portrait of a Village

Pughtown

By Maria Baird Garvin

I met my house in the aftermath of the huge snowstorm of February 1972. The day after the storm, my husband and I went for a ride to see how badly the landscape was ravaged. Our wandering took us out to Route 100 at Pughtown. Since routine trips generally did not take me west of the village of Birchrunville, where we rented our home, this was the first time I looked at Pughtown long enough to notice that it, too, was a village. My future home was on the left side of a rise across the highway from where we sat waiting to cross the intersection. Drifts of snow piled against the house's north wall, and the steps to the porch were no longer visible. The boughs of a huge white pine littered the front yard; several appeared to have been pushed off the roadway by plows the night before. There were no lights in the windows. The driveway was covered in knee-deep powder. I didn't know it for a long time afterward, but that morning the house had lost its beloved owner. As we sat, deciding on a route, I had time to gaze into those large, dark windows. At that moment, the house and I connected.

Villages are one of Pennsylvania's best-kept secrets. There are no road signs to point out when a traveler might be passing through one, nor do they appear on a typical road map, but they are very real. Many villages became this country's future cities and towns. Those that did not remained small, cohesive communities anchored by family or religion. Many Pennsylvania villages span the boundaries of more than one town or township, and some straddle county borders. The typical village is small, consisting of perhaps

The Diffendarfer House.

five to thirty families. Homes are situated together for sociability and defense, and land surrounding the living quarters is, for the most part, farmed. My love affair with villages began when, as a newly married couple, my husband and I rented an 1800s gristmill house in the village of Birchrunville. During the next six years, we continued to rent the mill and became a family of four and villagers. My two children had no end of grandparents, and several families treated me as though I was a daughter. From offering to watch the children for an afternoon to dropping off a few extra tomatoes from their garden, Birchrunville villagers treated my family as their own.

In the spring of 1972, we engaged a Realtor and, after much discussion, walked him around the village of Birchrunville in an effort to show him, not so much house styles, but the atmosphere we sought to find. We walked on small, rural roads to the general store and post office as I pointed out homes shared by two, sometimes three, generations. Many of the homes had small vegetable gardens outside the kitchen doors, clothes hanging on lines in the yard and dogs or cats asleep on the porch. I wanted a home with a sense of place, one that came with memories and neighbors who held essential values not abandoned in the name of progress. A place where church socials are still big events, where neighbors help with snow shoveling and where an afternoon of canning turns into an informal dinner party.

We looked at a lot of houses but connected with none of them. In April, our Realtor called and said he had an estate listing that might interest us and suggested I meet him at an intersection on Route 100 in front of the general store in Pughtown. I knew exactly where we were going. I had made it a point to drive through Pughtown and check up on that big, white house a number of times that spring. The windows remained dark and the yard unkempt.

The first indication of my future came when the Realtor opened the back door with a big, ornate key one associates with medieval churches. With the exception of indoor plumbing and a vintage electric stove, nothing in the house had been updated in over fifty years. The plumbing was in ruins. The pipes had frozen and burst when the large coal furnace in the basement shut down due to lack of fuel, which had occurred after the previous owner, Mr. Bill Montgomery, died of a heart attack while shoveling the walk to his garage following a big snow.

I stood in the kitchen feeling more like I was doing damage assessment than considering a place to bring Baird, my four-year-old son, and Lisa, his three-year-old sister, to live. The setting sun at my back, I looked into the large front hall, where a staircase beckoned further exploration. In the hazy half-light, the dark wood floors shone with a rosy hue. A faint smell of wood smoke pervaded the rooms, and everything was peaceful and quiet, as though the house were holding its breath. I felt safe and protected. The house was tendering an offer to us to become part of its history and its village. In response to that unspoken invitation, we signed the contract of sale that evening in the living room of our new home.

———◆———

Pughtown has changed little from over one hundred years ago. The church, feed store and hotel are all in the same locations. The houses themselves have changed very little. The people have changed even less. One will find names on mailboxes that still reflect the names on family plots in the cemetery. In fact, most of the houses in Pughtown are known by the name of their original owners. The town itself is named after one of its first settlers, John Pugh, who built there in the early 1700s on French Creek. My home stands adjacent to the Pugh estate and is known as the Henry Diffendarfer House.

With the plumbing repaired to the bank's satisfaction, we moved into our new house in June. Our major renovation that year was to replace the old coal furnace that only supplied heat to the first floor via grates with a modern heating system. Everything else remained as it had been for the past fifty years. My admiration for the housewives and mothers of previous generations grew as I struggled to prepare meals on the tiny stove shoved into a large walk-in fireplace. I did have a porcelain sink with a sideboard; however, there were no kitchen cabinets or counters, just a large windowsill. Until we were able to install a real kitchen, three years later, the large marble top of an ornate sideboard purchased at auction was my countertop: pots, pans, dishes and silverware were kept within the sideboard's cavernous doors and drawers.

Our hand-dug well supplied water via a belt-driven pump, which sounded, when running, like the *African Queen* making its way downriver. The Diffendarfer house had three bedrooms, a bathroom upstairs and three additional fireplaces. We also had a complete daughter-in-law apartment that was an addition to the south wall around 1880. It had two bedrooms, a fireplace, a bath, a living room and a large eat-in kitchen. The entire house had two of everything: attics, basements, enclosed porches previously known as summer kitchens, covered front and back porches and multiple doors.

Our house was built of fieldstone, as were most of the other homes from the same era in the village. At one point in its history, the Diffendarfer house was referred to as "The Philadelphia Cash House," or variety store, but for the most part, my house served as a home to a very short list of previous owners.

My first connection to the village's history came one morning, a month after we moved in, with a knock at the back door. Mina Bealer Caldwell, a woman of seventy-two and owner of the small stone house to the west of me on Daisy Point Road, had come to welcome the new family. She was a short woman with beautiful white hair cut in a classic pageboy. She wore an apron over her colorful housedress. Mina brought fresh eggs just gathered that morning and a basket of daffodil bulbs that were to be planted immediately. Mina was going to show me exactly where. After I learned she was Bill Montgomery's niece and had done all the planting on the property, I better understood her need to direct the placement of the daffodils. Her uncle Bill had been a bachelor all his life, and as he got older, she had taken on the domestic chores around the house for him. They watched out for each other, as both lived alone. Mina told me about the communication signals they had agreed on years ago. At five o'clock every evening, Bill would turn on his kitchen light, which she could see from her kitchen window. Mina would respond by lighting the lamp on her kitchen table, which could be seen from Bill's back door.

Up until her death in 1986, Mina was my history teacher. She was first introduced to the Diffendarfer house in 1919, when her grandfather, Hugh Montgomery, a local gristmill operator, purchased the house from John Blondin. Mina was nineteen years old at the time. In 1939, the house passed to Hugh's youngest son, Bill, and shortly after that, Mina purchased her home on Daisy Point Road. We were the "newer houses" in the village.

Our home first appeared on a deed in April 1835, when William Everhart conveyed to Henry Diffendarfer a stone house and a tract of seventy perches—which equals a bit more than one half acre. In 1835, there were a number of small industries flourishing on the west side of the village, including a wheelwright, a blacksmith, a shoemaker and a tailor. By this time, the hotel tavern, directly across from Diffendarfer's new purchase, on the east side of the Old Lenape Indian North/South Trail, presently Route 100, had already been operating a lucrative business for fifteen years. The hotel has since been converted into apartments, but its exterior has not changed in the least. On fine summer days, families sit out on the old hotel front porch, perhaps enjoying an after-dinner drink just as travelers might have taken the air over one hundred years ago after securing a room and a good meal.

Pughtown's history goes a long way back; the nucleus of the village had already taken shape by the early 1700s. Research indicates that three large

Pughtown.

tracts of land along the French Creek went to James Pugh and Simon Meridith from James Logan by way of an original land grant to Logan from William Penn. All of the northern section of Chester County was originally known as the "Skool Kill District" and included the three Coventry townships, as well as East and West Nantmeal.

When the children were young, I bought a reprint of a March 19, 1816 map of Chester County. The Pughtown crossroads is prominently noted as an established location within the township, known then as "the Coventries." My two children, who have fished French Creek since they could walk, can tell where every mill was located along its banks within the township of South Coventry. Finding a pile of fieldstones or what looked like a millrace, they used to run home to the map to try to identify what was once there.

—•—

I spent the first summer in our new home leading my house gently into the twentieth century. The décor, for the most part, was last changed around the time the house was purchased by Mr. Montgomery in 1939. One of the first things I noticed as I began the overdue spring cleaning and maintenance of the few plumbing and electrical updates the house did have was that Mr. Montgomery left notes everywhere. Neatly printed and dated missives, written on manila three-by-five shipping labels, hung on the item in question by a thin steel wire to remind him of things he had to do in the future or maybe to leave some kind of record for posterity. I found a note about the last time the belt on the water pump was changed, along with the proper size to order. Which storm window went with which window and what side faced out. I whispered a little "Thank you" when he made a chore easier. He and I had quite a few conversations in those early years. He watched over my shoulder, making sure I followed his instructions to the letter. The notes were tangible proof of my house's history, and my family continued to contribute to that history. It became a habit of my husband's and mine to add the next date an item was serviced or replaced, as well as any helpful additional notes, right to Bill's originals.

There were other records as well. In many of the rooms, upon removing the wallpaper, I found a signature and the date the room was last papered in large and perfect Palmer script. Starting with the living room, the first date I discovered was 1950. Excited, I called Mina over to show her. Seeing it, she became a bit pensive and ran home to "find something." She returned with a large envelope and a story. Mina married in 1950, and Bill had offered his house for the reception. In return for this kindness, Mina agreed to spruce up his downstairs and paper the living room. She chose a floral pattern of large blue roses. On the day before Mina started the wallpaper project, Bill signed and dated the newly prepared living room wall. After telling the story, she opened the envelope and showed me her wedding pictures.

Black-and-white photographs from 1950, taken in my living room in its newly papered splendor. She and her new husband posed in front of the fireplace, which looked exactly the same as it does now, sixty years later. That afternoon, I was regaled with a short history of every person in her wedding party. In one of her pictures, I saw a large professional photograph of Hugh Montgomery, Bill's father, hanging in an ornate oval frame between the two front windows over a Victorian sofa. Mina and I found the outline of that frame, still visible, on the faded blue paper. And I met Bill Montgomery. Unsmiling, in formalwear, Bill appeared stern in the wedding photographs, but his eyes were kind. Now I had a face to go with the conversations I carried on with him while scraping off the old wallpaper, sanding miles of baseboard and window trim and scrubbing the fine patina of coal dust from everything not already scraped or sanded.

Mina shared her family history with me freely. Her past, complete with pictures and old newspaper articles, suddenly became part of my daily life. Mina shared it all, the happy times as well as the sad ones. Many of her stories, especially those about her mother and late husband, she recited on our occasional walks to the cemetery beside the Pughtown Baptist Church. With Mina as my tour guide, we walked through the rows of tombstones that anchored her stories with names and dates carved in stone.

History wasn't all I learned. The original village houses were built before electricity, central heat and indoor plumbing were parts of everyday life. Houses were oriented to take advantage of natural light, placing bedrooms and kitchens where they would be lit and warmed by the sun when occupied. The south side of the houses usually had few windows, and the walk-in fireplace was also generally built on that wall, since that side of the house was exposed to the higher summer sun. Every room, as well as the stairwells, had a door, which seemed a bit much to me at first. But after I learned how to control the air flow through the house by the judicious opening and closing of doors, I realized I would be lost without them. The house design lent itself to natural air conditioning. The secret was using hot air's natural tendency to rise to pull cool air in from the outside in the evening. As the hot air rose, it gained momentum, flowing up the circular staircases, built one on top of another from basement to attic, and exiting out a window at the very top of the attic steps. Cooling off the house in this manner and then shutting it off from the outside early in the morning allowed the house to be ten degrees cooler inside during the summer. Our forefathers planned and designed their houses to work with nature. Living in a village and taking time to understand these houses has taught three generations of my family how to combine centuries-old methods with modern technology to provide a comfortable, less expensive and healthier environment.

A few of the home's enhancements, standard one hundred years ago, lent themselves to more modern purposes. The summer kitchen made a wonderful laundry room with easy access to the clothesline in the side yard, and we equipped all the fireplaces with woodstoves to provide supplemental heat.

Three generations of my family live in Henry Diffendarfer's old house. After my son Baird married in the early '90s, he moved into our daughter-in-law suite. His new family lived here with their daughter, Victoria, until they were able to afford their first home. My husband passed away in 1996, and it was then that my daughter Lisa decided she wanted to raise her children in a village. I moved about eighteen inches south, and the daughter-in-law suite became the mother-in-law suite. What this house lacked in closets it certainly made up for in versatility.

I see now, with perfect clarity, that our founding fathers built for their families', as well as their country's, future. They designed their homes to accommodate children, marriages and, when needed, the aging parent. Pughtown has several households consisting of more than one generation. In the rare instance a village house is offered for sale, it is the house that chooses its new owner.

The old stone home that belonged to Mina just west of me changed hands again recently. The house prefers single women and is partial to chickens. True to form, its new owner turned out to be a single, young woman. In the spring of 2011, one year shy of forty years after I first met Mina, that new owner walked up the path to my house with a basket of freshly gathered eggs. I thanked her, and after a long pause, she told me that every evening, about five o'clock, she found herself glancing up at our house with a sense of anticipation. She admitted she had no idea why or even what she was looking for but that when our kitchen lights finally came on, she knew she was where she belonged.

Each Revolution Would

Collegeville

By Adam Haller

From without, it appeared the house suffered cataracts. The brick façade masked its upper half in softly faded green aluminum siding. The windows held screens and frosted panes, and behind them, stapled to the painted sheetrock of each room, the 6 Mil sheeting blinked in vague recognition against the drafts of winter. In one of these windows on the second floor, a boy worked the staples from the drywall with the otherwise useless file of his nail clippers. He peeled back the lower corner of the plastic, blew away the evidence and attempted to make out snowflakes.

He replaced the staples in their dual holes, and on the brown shag carpet of the hall, his determined steps fell without sound. More than one weatherman confessed the possibility of snow, enough to buy into promise.

Downstairs, he filled the kerosene heaters with shimmering viscous liquid from the canister through the orange-capped siphon. He and his younger brother watched *Happy Days* reruns. Mom made a meatloaf and mashed potatoes. Dad finished the customer calls and began the Conshohocken commute. At home, he had Coke with ice, kicked back in his recliner to watch the Flyers with his sons. Hextall glared through the twenty-nine-inch screen; he slapped the posts and skated his crease. The house door remained unlocked till morning, and the keys were more like spares. The family inside—the mother and father, the sleeping daughter, the two rapt sons—confederated and armed in refuge against wind howls and the streetlight's crisp electrical hum, watched.

It was 1989 in Montgomery County, 7:35 in the dark evening.

He let his boys watch the first period, said, "Time for bed" and the two brothers went upstairs to brush their teeth. They scampered off to shiver under covers until the game's tension and volume rose.

The kerosene sprites settled over them, and they smiled hard when Dad yelled, "Ho!" They hunched over the air-vent tunnel leading down to the living room, clenching fists, grabbing night-shirted shoulders, the tees Dad wore driving truck across the states. Emerick and Clement's play-by-play graced the ductwork and careened upward, almost unhindered. Prostrate on the coarse shag, pressing ears to the conduit to their team and their father, they looked at each other imbued with everything enshrined in the word "brother." Listening, they cramped and stretched and curled and drowsed into icy dreams.

They woke. Outside, the world, less mottled, glowed as the faint sun reflected still brighter on the ground. Stretching the plastic for confirmation, for solace, they knew the reward of believing in slim odds. They had a day in which they tossed time's choke-chain on the homework and it played no factor.

⋯•⋯

Back in '95, a hell of a blizzard did anything but creep in. Breathless blizzards blew in upon the already dead and buried blizzards wheezing and sputtering in sheet-white snow. School closed for days at a time—twelve and a half years old and granted liberation.

We grew up in a neighborhood on a hill with maple-lined streets, enough fields to run with dogs in the belief we were wholly rural, ample parking lots to make over into Spectrum ice when the snow wasn't three feet deep. But if so, we invented new games by jumping off the back deck until the plows came, into three feet of snow, twisting in the air and puffing down in the quiet between the blanketed ground and the thick wet-cotton clouds. We lounged in the sound of snow falling on snow already fallen.

We hated school, and when the forecast called for snow, sleep became stubborn. My brother slid downstairs in his one-piece zip-up pajamas and hit the front door just as I rounded the rail into the small dining room and attached kitchen. With KYW news radio ten-sixty, Mom and Dad drank coffee. We attempted to resolve the man through the wires to our side of the argument by reciting the merits of snow days. I'd say, "Tomato soup and grilled cheese." My brother would say, "Swiss Miss," and I'd add, "Marshmallows." We pleaded with him to cancel. He worked his way through each Delaware Valley county school district. Updates and bulletins crashed behind him. We debated outcomes until he got to *M*, and we all had to be real quiet then and pray—in the silent, magical way that earned us a dog for Christmas. "Montgomery County," the man said, and we prayed. "Parochial Schools." We thanked God we didn't have to wear uniforms, didn't know why Mom wished she could afford St. Mary's when Mass on Sunday was enough. "Public Schools." We listened, they listened. "Perkiomen Valley School District," we heard, and it was true. It all came true. It was time to go get Eddie, time to go sledding, time for cold to needle our lungs and paint us red.

Seasons dictated our games. We went from football and hockey to spring, in which we grabbed bats and tennis balls, our gloves and called out who we were. "I'm Mike Schmidt." "No, you got to be Mike Schmidt last time." "Well, I'm Cal Ripken." We wore away all the grass seed Dad put down— and by the time the nights lengthened into summer, the rain muddied an infield-shaped triangle of dirt.

The author and his brother as boys fishing Green Lane Reservoir.

We played by archaic rules, by glory and danger, altering many of them to favor the off-chance of brutality. The hitter could be thrown out on strikes, the runner forced out at base or, due to a lack of fielders, pegged in the back of the head. Our preferred method left the opponent slinking back to the on-deck sidewalk with a welt. But if the runner, careful enough, agile and lucky enough, could duck, jump or otherwise twist his way from the missile, he neutralized the fielder, left him fuming at the jig invented at his expense by the runner on the easy path to home. If unlucky, sliding headfirst into third, the runner might be plunked squarely in the left testicle, with a game-ending out, finding himself recuperating with an ice pack on the couch.

We fished and swam in the summer, turned rocks for crayfish and grub, constructed for weeks Schuylkill-bound rafts finally abandoned in fights. Though without fail, by the time we returned to one another, even in a day's time, from the short-lived bitterness of given-up projects, we conceived new ones. Our chief inertia, in those stretched-out days, was the river. The Perky, muddy enough to conceal sea monsters in its depth yet shallow enough in places to wade. The Indian-christened Perkiomen, whose name stood for eradication, trailed like a tired dragon through our dreams of vanished civilizations.

On such a summer day, inside for lunch, a stranger arrived trenched in shadows. My brother and I identified him, pacing the sidewalk and approaching the lawn. He looked, not at the trees, though he touched their bark, but at the house. He was after something, escaped from Graterford Prison and hostage shopping. "You just don't look at a house that way," we thought. We pointed him out, feared him.

"Oh, he's probably buying in the neighborhood," Mom said. The man approached and we scrambled, yelled to warn her. He knocked. She answered, and we listened from behind the door, stealing peeks into the slant light outside, glimpses of his face. He apologized as if the crime had already been committed. She said it was nothing and invited him in. We hated him and his ruse instantly.

We followed his motions, at a three-foot distance, for tells. He didn't even take off his shoes, and we had to take off ours and put them in a bench by the front door. He looked at the sill that would function as a parapet. The featureless man loomed in our hallways. He jostled the loose railing Mom yelled at us for. He crested the landing and lowered his shoulders, straightened them and looked at the ceiling and then down the hall. My mother motioned for him. We followed them down the hall.

"This is the boys' room."

"All three of them in here?" he said, for there were three boys now. "It was just the two of us," he said, "my brother and me."

So, he was after neither mark nor hostage; the realization stung us. He eyed the molding. As a boy, to him, they were like whale ribs. He tried the door hinge, stooped to the windowpane. His silence and wonderment stayed until after he should have acknowledged it, being such an alteration to grasp. At last, he shook his head and guessed the place had always been this small.

"The new deck is certainly different," he said.

This is our house, and we do what we want to make it better. You don't get to say what is different. Your deck was a bread line for termites. We have a new grill. And Mom says we are tearing up the stupid puke-brown shag rug in our bedroom. We knew then, with certainty, the house had known others before us, had sheltered and reared them. He could drive anywhere, and this was his choice to come here. I pitied him and felt disdain.

People lived through things. They got old and forgot. Then, too late, they tried to remember everything that happened. What else could drag a grown man back with so much worry in tow? I learned this, and I wanted no part of it. The whole point was to grow up. So I devised to write it all down, every night before bed. Monday morning, I asked Mom for thirty-five cents to buy a tan composition book from my teacher. I would write it all down so I would never have to come back.

Years later, and by the time Mom took work at the nursing home a few towns over, we considered ourselves young men. With each year, the place smelled more pungent, the sight of it more bitter for what it took out of her and what it exacted from the patients in their last and lonesome moments of life, for the crime they committed of dragging it out.

When licensed to drive, my brother and me, we'd pick Mom up at eleven or drop her off at eleven so we could have the car. Of her other wards, we knew only oblique details. Edgar, whose cancer-cleft ears looked like a schizoid knife-virgin wore the surgeon's gloves on operation day. Down the shore each summer after that, as if in homily, Mom reminded us of Edgar, and we soaped with SPF against the looming and patient death in us.

No story, however, of Carl and his emphysema mask could keep us from turning spiteful and callous toward her examples, as we stood by the pay phone of the under-new-management mart with three loose ones for a bad enough looking customer to buy us smokes and not give us shit. All my intentions pointed away.

⟞•⟝

Up river—and why it, the Perky, by August, trickled—was Green Lane reservoir. We could rent boats and plaster our shoes with goose shit. There later, with our own car, we'd think about our father in an aura of worm bait. How we hated to fish with them, but Dad, with a badge of pragmatism, would use boot leather if he thought it'd put a fish on the line. Where they dammed the Perky was a monument for us, and on its time-scarred face we saw the years between fishing with Pop and stealing boats and tossing bottles. It was not 1985, but I drove that year's Chevy Blazer. It leaked oil like a sieve after a day of dishwashing, straining the pulp and stems from unfinished cocktails. The under-hood tattooed with stains from spouted brake fluid and when the water pump went up. At the Exxon, I asked Annie how she's been, like it wasn't her name I knifed in a tree on the banks in sixth grade. The back seat folded down for plywood but had yet to see a lost flower. Also, the mechanism that might have locked the bench in its upright position didn't work, so whenever I pumped the brakes and prayed to God they worked, friends had to hold on, and on morning rides to school, my sister white-knuckled the headrest to keep from the windshield. Winter brought me early to warm it, and even then, there was no heat, so we bundled for the drive, wiping breath-fog from the windshield with hunting gloves. Dad paid $300 for her, but she was worth more, and special— both of us born with a respect for Springsteen cassettes—special for she labored the lot of us northward to the reservoir.

By then, we were miles away from where we had been. Green Lane, our star, where though we hurtled about on the dizzy world, each revolution would bring us back to the reservoir, where we rowed out to the tranquil middle, photo-like save for mosquito ripples and the slurp of rising bass and the roil of the fat-greased carp. We'd drop anchor—a coffee can filled with concrete, held to the sand and the grass in the dark under-hull. We stared at water where ancient stars and moons, through atmospheric shimmer, reflected near perfection, leaned back when the conversation lulled to watch space dust burning as they trespassed where we breathed. People call them shooting stars, but they aren't. We drifted on the same water; continue to, the disparate sons that we are.

Every so often, the boy I'd been speaks as if he pities me for not noticing gifts. He says, Where have you been? You promised not to but keep doing what makes you forget. Remember the farmer owned a wild field that stood between us and the drugstore's candy aisle. We crossed to town by way of the ravine, climbed on all fours, scampered up chair-sized boulders, footholds few. Eddie grabbed your hand just as his ground gave way to a mossy mine shaft and snarling hounds of pain below yelped curses.

There was a sound like when you stick your fingers in your ears that was your blood.

We hid beneath the shin-rippers and briars. When we leapt and tripped and jumped and slipped in our run to make the sanctuary of the road, we heard the report of the farmer's twelve-gauge as we bested his intimidations with gregarious agility. We turned rocks in his milkweed and kept as pets his garter snakes and ringnecks that grew five feet, and we set them free by the stream of spiders and water-walkers, pollen-white in some slow pools. We built forts in tree roots the spring winds tore from earth and swung from vines hanging down from hundred-year oaks.

In the woods, we were certain of mystery.

Mr. Miles, who closed on Sunday, hired pretty young girls, princesses with plastic nametags. He also had penny candy and five-cent candy, so no matter how hard up we were or how many chores we skipped, we could always get a Now & Later to last until dinner. We braved the Farmer's Field with folded dollars in our socks, and when we hit pavement, we'd remove sweaty shoes to get at the coins between our toes. But that top magazine rack occupied an increasing portion of our thoughts. Then came the breaking point; we grabbed a magazine, the gang scurried, a single entity of grafted boy, down an empty aisle, huddled—sex splayed out spread eagle on glossy, air-brushed pages. Rearranging bulges, we laughed at boobies and unbeknownst crossed other ravines.

You still have the scars from gang warfare, huh? Factions of neighborhood boys owning little neighborhood nations, learning of illusory peace, borders, hate for no reason. Once, the enemy hit our brother with a tube sock full of ice, blindsided him on the temple. He went down. And in a rage you try not to feel ever, you straddled, punched and screamed in murder. Years this went on, until one of their captains fell off the water tower and had a closed casket. We didn't fight much after that. When we heard the news, our vengeance said, "Good."

Could have turned out differently, couldn't it? That time I walked away from the gaggle, my friends who surrounded Sadie, lifting up her skirt to reveal real girl parts to boys who'd only ever seen owned parts. Everybody giggled and punched one another to hush. And I put my arms up to the highest branch of a maple and pulled my legs up by my skinny arms, couldn't help to look back. It meant simple things were over for good. I knew she did it and didn't want to.

You stole smokes from ashtrays all over the North Atlantic. At fifteen, you'd smoke anything. You raided ashtrays outside stores and supped from butts with lipstick smacked on. You did disgusting things. The guillotine fell in the time it took all the moons to shear from full to new. That was your goodbye.

The boy, he brings these things to mind.

—◆—

The move came, and like those with premonitions of larger diaspora, my family took with us more than we should. Dad drove the brim-filled U-Haul, I the tarp-roped Chevy pickup, fifteen years' worth. The trash men had no idea what awaited, rattling up our hill. Twice, before departure, I chased neighborhood day-orphans, bent on destruction and armed with bludgeons, from our dump-bound wares. Our insides, what we had used and no longer had use for, exposed, a fish tank of what we left behind.

I knew this chill before, with my father watching ice shards ride the flooding Perkiomen. Under Mom's bed, in a shoebox of pictures, freezing water eclipses bridges and road signs, snow and ice-melt fill the valley. On that day, we got out of the car and watched our river become violent with early season rain. Volunteer firemen backed us up. We watched damn fools cross the warning. It would calm, we knew, as we had calmed from the

Gravel Pike and the road to Graterford Prison with floodwaters.

violence between us, but rage is truly a sight. There was always some fool to drown. In a couple days, he'd be in the paper, and we all knew someone who knew him. With this man's name arrived mortal thoughts. We felt that day proud of what was ours as we witnessed the possessions of others float away. What more so qualifies a thing as loved? How hard we fight to save it or how it is envisioned when we can't bring it back.

I considered this and more driving northbound on 95 to Gravel Pike and 29. The burnished dogwood rose higher than the house, and its existence was due to the now anonymous family that was. We planted it on Mother's Day. In the neighborhood, there are the Goths that made good—job, house, child steering battery-driven Hot Wheels ahead of them, already disrespectful of their authority, nursing a spite that has but to grow, for a mother and father as yet tethered to black shirts, ink and piercings glittering Elmer's Glue skin. Another woman pushes a stroller and gives a cautious hello, gauging the molester threat level. "I used to live here," I say. She nods, and her smile says that *is* what you would say.

The house had known new improvers, new glass and weather seal to guard all within against the drafts, the heat and massed recollections of yet another prodigal charge, another featureless man. The upstairs window aimed across the lot and street to the playground. Other elbows lean on its sill, another one, a one of many, who says, "I am Chase Utley, I'm Ryan Howard," who hangs from branches by skinny arms, orders wiz-with, waits in the bedroom window for the streetlight to illuminate tomorrow's forecasted snow, hammers a decking board or gets pushed down a grassy hill without training wheels, who disregards his mother's *Love You* Post-it stuck to a brown-bagged ham and cheese.

Here eight years returned from all the moves since, looking at the corner window of the town house on Salem that could not placate my dreams of other lands. I pace the yard, a zoo creature, cordoned off from my previous world, now inhabited by others who dub me stranger. Here is the grass that stained me, the maple propellers we split and adorned ourselves with, the curbs we sat on, the sidewalk, the street itself where we left blood and knee skin, the streetlights that signaled the end of youthful play, the clouds that painted for us. I had studied ants and plotted dreams in the pathways of them all.

Our home blurred through kerosene fumes and plastic and became what it was. I did not even ascend the curb or kneel to my old field. My previous life came to me in stabs. Something unassailable happened here and will not be happened upon again.

Sepia Memories

Trappe/Upper Providence Township

By Stacey Ziegler Harp

I held a nail, gripped between thumb and forefinger, as close to the wall as I possibly could. Swinging the hammer toward the nail head, I held my breath, hoping I wouldn't miss. Though tools and I have never gotten along, I had, against my better judgment, volunteered to hang my wedding photo for my mother.

The hammer hit squarely, driving the nail. I picked up the frame and secured the wire on the hook. Dropping my hands to the lower corners of the frame, I made sure the picture was level.

The photo, a black-and-white image of my husband and me embracing, the top of my head barely meeting the top of his shoulder, looked elegant in its silver frame. I love this photograph. Black-and-white photos seem flawless; the gray tones soften the marks and wrinkles of life and add an air of old-time glamour.

Next to my newly hung picture was the photograph of my great-grandparents Earl and Margaret Bechtel, a sepia image framed in simple brown wood that had stared down at me from the same spot since childhood. Their photo always begged me to stop to look whenever I passed by.

Earl, or Pop, stood in his three-piece suit, jacket buttoned, his hat in hand, his dark brown hair brushed across his forehead by his fingers. Margaret, or Mammie, wore a double-breasted cloth "slouch" coat with velvet cuffs and oversized buttons, her head topped with a broad-brimmed hat. She clutched a small satin purse in her gloved hand. Looking into the sun, their

Earl Poley Bechtel and Margaret Kulp Keeley, going to get married, October 12, 1915. Taken at Margaret's parents' home on Betcher Road in Upper Providence Township, Pennsylvania.

eyes squint in the glare, smiles play on their faces. They are a few inches apart, Pop's arm behind Mammie's waist their only physical contact. It's a beautiful photo, taken outside Mammie's mother's home on Betcher Road in Upper Providence. After many years of admiring that photo, I discovered it was their wedding photo.

While preparing for our wedding a year ago, Dave and I thought since we both came from close families, we wanted to include elements from each of them. We decided we would use family wedding photographs to decorate our cake table. When I asked my mother if there was one of my great-grandparents, she informed me that the photograph that had hung outside my bedroom my entire life was their wedding photo.

Sure enough, when I removed the picture from the frame to make a copy, on the back, scrawled in faded pencil, it read "Earl and Margaret—Going to get married. October 12, 1915." I was startled to know that this was the single picture to document their special day.

Earl and Margaret were born in Upper Providence Township, part of the Perkiomen Valley in Pennsylvania at the turn of the twentieth century. Life was brutal, work never-ending and money hard to come by, but they were resilient people who lived into their nineties and enjoyed not only their grandchildren but their great-grandchildren as well.

I remembered Mammie smiling, her arms outstretched with a plate of the vanilla sandwich cookies my four-year-old stomach couldn't get enough of in the sunny white kitchen at the back of their house on Greenwood Avenue in Trappe. Pop in their living room, his rotund body snugly perched in a small armchair, sat ready to share his stories. He loved to tell stories and had even taken the time when he was in his eighties to painstakingly record them on an ancient typewriter. A rough task to accomplish at any age, but at eighty, to record 115 pages of one's life by typing with just two fingers on each hand, is an incredible feat. Even Pop understood his struggle, and throughout his memoir, he would beg his audience forgiveness for errors, omissions or lack of a chronological story.

The fact is that while writing this I am continually thinking of some episode that I should have mentioned earlier. Also, as I am a very slow and miserable typist, typing this at least twice and some of it three or four times has been, to say the least, a prodigious task. The task of reediting and retyping the entire script, is appalling to say the least.

Though he struggled, Pop gave us his stories forever. As I stared at the two different wedding photos, his words came back to me.

It was the year 1915 and Margaret and I are considering marriage. What colossal optimism, or was it just plain ignorance? I had less than $200 cash with which to finance this important step. Certainly a person with any common sense would label such a decision foolhardy, to say the least.

Much to my surprise, when I informed Dad that we were getting married, he did not mention finances, which were always his chief concern, his only comment was; "Don't you think you are making a mistake? Margaret is too delicate."

I often wonder what Pop's father meant by that comment. Too delicate? For what? Farm work? Life? To be his daughter-in-law? In his mind it was probably a combination of all those things. Mammie was not too delicate. She was a rather tall woman for that time, standing somewhere around five feet, five inches, and firmly built. Even in her wedding photo, she stands near Pop, looking very much his equal in size and stature. Her mother, Sallie, was widowed when Mammie was only eighteen months old. Sallie's husband died of tuberculosis, and when she remarried, Sallie chose a farmer. Mammie was her mother's daughter, strong in body and will, and grew up farming. In Pop's own words, life on the farm was not easy, but it is something Mammie would have been able to handle with ease.

The life of a farmer's wife was an extremely busy one, particularly during the months of May through December. Early in May she was busy preparing and planting the garden and truck patch. Planting every type of vegetable, not only for summer use but to preserve and store for winter consumption as well.

June brought pail after pail of luscious strawberries, raspberries, and blackberries. Now the farm kitchen became a veritable furnace, which continued through most of the summer, making jars and jars of preserves.

When the garden began to mature, peas, beans, and other vegetables and fruits had to be processed. Those that could not be canned or preserved had to be dried, or salted for preservation, particularly corn and beans.

In late October winter apples were ripe and ready for picking. They were stored in barrels or bins in the cellar or a cave, if one was available. When the apples were harvested, many were dropped and would have to be used promptly or they would spoil. They were gathered up and pressed into cider, though not to drink. It would be stored in barrels to be turned into vinegar or made into apple butter by the farm wife.

I have never been able to figure out why Pop's father, Oliver, would have made such a statement about Mammie, but it was most likely only out of spite. He was, by all accounts, a bastard, treating those around him with utter cruelty. Our family's abhorrence of him was so great that we still tell stories about him. My mother, though almost ten years old when he died, only remembers that he pinched, and she hated to go near his room at Mammie and Pop's, where he lived during the declining years of his life. Even decades later, she has no pictures of him in her mind.

Pop wrote a story about Oliver that has become infamous in our family and is used to depict his true character when people question whether we are exaggerating his personality.

Quite some years before, Mother had one breast removed, malignant, of course. We had hopes that this would halt the spread of disease but she developed breathing difficulties and soon could only breathe with the help of oxygen. At the time, Mother and Dad, were living with my sister Mildred and her husband Charlie. Mother was confined to her bed for months and had to have a nurse with her, continually. This was quite an expense, which was a source of great concern to Dad, who wanted to put her in a hospital. He talked it over with me one day and I said "No!" in no uncertain terms. I told him; "You know very well that she will never come back and she is going to stay with her family for what little time she has left." So she remained at Charlie and Mildred's home, along with Dad.

I always made it a point to stop for a short visit with her on my way home, if at all possible. At the head of the stairway was a landing and here Mildred had a small desk and a chair. Mother's room was just to the right, with the door opening on this landing. Mother had a clear view of this desk, as she lay in bed. When I came up, there was Dad with his account book, a look of intense worry on his face, stroking his head and totaling up his expenses. I cannot help but believe that this was one of the prime reasons why Mother begged the doctor to give her something to put her to sleep.

Pop was blessed to have a mother that he adored and who adored him in return, but both suffered under the cruelty of spirit that raged in Oliver. In reading sections of Pop's memoirs, I am overwhelmed by the feelings of sympathy I have for Pop's mother, Anna, though I was not lucky enough to ever know her.

When I first read Pop's description of his wedding day, I was amazed to find that there was not a single family member to witness their ceremony. Pop hooked up his horse, Prince, to the buggy and drove to Betcher Road to pick up Mammie. They took a single photograph and rode together to Augustus Lutheran Church.

> *Margaret and I were on our way to the parsonage, the memory of that beautiful day is still with me. The sky was bright and beautiful, with great white clouds like ships in full sail on an azure sea, we proceed out Seventh Avenue.*
>
> *Mrs. Fegley and "Auntie" Fegley, gave us a warm welcome and witnessed the ceremony. Dr. Fegley pronounced the benediction. We were then man and wife and on our way home.*

They were married on a Tuesday afternoon in October in Augustus Lutheran Church's parsonage. The minister officiated in his living room, with his wife and daughter to witness the event. The church, just steps away, was not where they made their sacred promises to each other. I asked my mother once why they weren't married in the church and why it was on a Tuesday afternoon. She wasn't sure, but she thought based on Pop's stories that they simply went when they could find the time. Oliver was as harsh a farm owner as he was a father and a husband, forcing Pop to do all the work at the farm, so it was not often that Pop had any free time. They had to go when he had a few hours to himself.

Not one person, not one family member or friend, was there to stand for my great-grandparents or witness their promises to each other. They had no parents to bless their union. Mammie's father, dead when she was less than two years old, wasn't there to walk her down the aisle. There was no aisle. Her mother, unable to abandon her farm, now short one person, even for a few hours, wasn't there to fix her hair or kiss her on the cheek. When their ceremony was over, they simply went home. There was no celebration. No toast, no dancing, no cake.

Our ceremony was the exact opposite of my great-grandparents' simple, quick one. We had six bridesmaids, six groomsmen and almost three hundred guests looking on as I walked down the long aisle with my arm through my father's to "Here Comes the Sun." Our bridal party, in painstakingly chosen coordinating colors, stood behind us as we exchanged our vows on an unseasonably warm day in March. We processed and recessed to live music. We had a minister, which leant an air of religion to our outdoor, nonreligious service.

My wedding culminated in a party worthy of such a special occasion. We served crab cakes, mini peanut butter and jelly sandwiches, a mashed potato bar with all the fixings, boardwalk French fries, Kobe beef sliders. We had an open bar to make sure no one went thirsty and four different flavors of cake. We had live music and dancing for four hours. We had speeches given by our brothers and best friends. It was a party that was still being talked about a year later.

> *I shall always cherish the memory of Mother standing at the door, as we approached the house, her arms outstretched, gathering Margaret into her arms in a loving welcome.*

Pop's mother was home, alone, during his wedding ceremony. While Anna had the same responsibilities as any farm wife, she had an advantage that Mammie's mother did not; she was gaining another set of helping hands just a few hours later. It would have been easy for Anna to come witness the short ceremony of her only son. Long after Pop died, I remember asking my grandfather why Anna hadn't attended Mammie and Pop's wedding if she was home. He merely said that Oliver probably wouldn't let her.

Earl and Margaret's home at 94 Greenwood Avenue, Upper Providence Township, Pennsylvania, as it looked when it was completed in 1925. Taken from their "truck patch" at the back of the house.

I can't imagine not having my parents or Dave's parents at our wedding. They were, and still are, the most important people in our lives. To hold such a monumental event without them would have been impossible.

After our wedding, Dave and I left on our honeymoon. Ten days of peace and bliss in Aruba. We sat on the beach, soaking up more sun than we had seen throughout the entire Pennsylvania winter. We explored caves filled with paintings and names carved by ancient hands. Food, drink, relaxation and adventure filled our days and nights.

As so frequently happened, whenever I was involved in something of unusual significance something would come up. My wedding day was no exception. It happened that Dad was up at Shall Cross in Schwenksville, helping them fill the silo that day, leaving me with all the barn chores, which meant spending the first three hours of my honeymoon in the cow stable.

A simple ceremony, no celebration or honeymoon, just a short ride through Trappe in a horse and buggy. One photo to document the occasion and nearly seventy years of marital happiness.

Reflecting on the contrast between this simple ceremony and that of our grandchildren, I wonder, can their marriages, possibly be any happier than ours has been? My prayers have always been; may their lives be as long and happy as ours. I could ask no more.

Waiting with the Holsteins

Wrightstown

By Rebecca Helm Beardsall

The Pennsylvania State Grange is the state's largest rural-farm organization. Organized in 1867 as a farm fraternity, the Grange represents citizens in 550 rural communities and is chartered in 55 of PA's 67 counties.

The opening ceremonies of the Middletown Grange Fair started with the national anthem and the raising of the American flag, the Grange flag and the 4-H flag. People walked to the aluminum bleachers and asked, "What's going on here?" pointing at the show ring. I told them the dairy judging was starting. Most said okay and either found a seat or walked away in search of cotton candy or French fries. One gentleman asked, "How do they judge dairy cows? Is it on how much milk they produce?" The man in front of me started to answer, "Udders," but I chimed in.

"These are heifers," to which I received a blank stare. "Heifers aren't milk producing."

"But I thought this was dairy judging."

"It is. But these are heifers."

"City slickers," I thought to myself as the gentlemen continued discussing udders. I went back to studying the dairy program. Funny, here I was, far from a farm girl—I didn't grow up on a farm, I just had farmers in the family—and I'm calling this guy a city slicker. For all I know, he lives in the same development as me and my husband.

The announcer called in the Spring Heifer Class programs, and pens clicked as the judging began. I'd been waiting for the moment the first hoof hit the wood chips.

I tried to guess which heifer would win first place. I studied their backs: are they long and straight? I looked at the angles, the size from end to end and the balance of the individual cow. But above all, I enjoyed watching the waltz taking place in the ring. Instead of a shiny dance floor, the participants have absorbent wood chips.

The handlers are dressed in all white—a dairy tradition that perhaps goes back to the milkman delivery days. The dance begins as the handler walks backward into the ring leading the heifer. When a heifer steps out of line, the handler must get her back in the procession by walking her in a small, tight circle. These little circles create a lovely diversion to the larger circle's little pirouettes. The handler must be an adroit dancer; in addition to presenting the heifer by walking in line, he or she must be able to dodge the piss and shit. The constant push, pull, dodge creates the robust waltz that could only be performed in a dairy judging ring. And the judge stands all the while in the middle of the circle, like the childhood game Farmer in the Dell, deciding on whom to pick first.

I last went to the Grange Fair in 1991, when I watched my brother Dwayne and his team prepare his heifers for the ring and place in judging. A self-employed dairy farmer, he couldn't stay on site because he still needed to milk his herd twice a day. The Middletown Grange was twenty minutes away from his farm, Morning Glory Holsteins in Pipersville. That year, my younger cousin Seth spent a month on the farm with my brother, and Dwayne brought him along to help at the Grange Fair. Seth's first exposure to dairy cows started in the big white barn on Dwayne's farm, and Seth was thrilled to work alongside my brother. Dwayne was in his element and used each moment to teach Seth something about the Holstein breed. The same year my brother was elected to the board of directors of the Pennsylvania Holstein Association as the Bucks County representative.

In 1992, the Middletown Grange Fair was dedicated to Dwayne's memory; he had passed away earlier that year. He fell into the feed mixer after the evening milking, causing multiple injuries to his neck, chest and legs. The 1992 program read, "The show committee of the Bucks County Holstein Club would like to dedicate the 1992 show to the late Dwayne Helm…Dwayne Helm was a frequent participant in this show, and due to his untimely death, he will be deeply missed." Though I was living in Scotland during the 1992 Grange Fair, I did see pictures of Tracey, my brother's widow, handing out the championship awards.

Award-winning rabbit at the 2010 Middletown Grange Fair, Wrightstown, Pennsylvania.

On August 20, 2010, my parents and I drove south to Wrightstown to attend the Middletown Grange Fair for my first time since my brother died. When we arrived early in the morning, the vendors had yet to open their tents. The crowing of roosters and the cries of the sheep directed me to the barns and livestock pavilions on the fairgrounds. The first barn I entered housed the chickens, rabbits and goats. I've always been a sucker for rabbits. Every time I see one of those little furry faces, I decide I need to have a rabbit. These decisions, in the past, usually resulted in me walking into my family's house with a large box and a rabbit or two. This year, I left the fairgrounds bunny-less.

Rabbits. The first animal my brother decided to raise. At the height of the bunny phase, we had three rabbit hutches in our backyard in downtown Quakertown. The first rabbit Dwayne brought home was a chocolate brown Rex rabbit he bought to show and breed. I wanted to name her, and my brother let me: Brownie. The next rabbit I named Grayie; the male rabbit, Whitey. One spring day, the white rabbit beat up beautiful little Brownie. As usual, I was tagging along with my brother when he opened the white rabbit's cage and told me to stand guard. I stood, arms straight out in front of the hutch door; nothing was going to get past me. Looking over my shoulder I asked, "What are you doin'?"

He tapped his baseball hat, which already sat above his head in typical farmer fashion, and looked at me over his plastic glasses frames. "Well, Chubs, I'm going to stick Brownie in there with Whitey and hopefully we will get bunnies."

"Bunnies!" I was so excited.

Whitey wasn't willing to play along. The fur started flying the moment Dwayne placed Brownie in the cage. She backed up into the corner as Whitey reared back and slashed his claws into her fur. The whole cage rocked as he rammed into the walls. He abused Brownie as she wiggled her butt into the corner to become smaller. I learned rabbits could screech. Dwayne had to separate them before Whitey killed Brownie. I stood frozen, but Dwayne laughed at me. "I don't think they like each other," he said as he checked Brownie's scratches before gently placing her back in her hutch.

My brother's clan of rabbits sparked a rabbit adopting tradition in our family that lasted until 1997, when my mom gave away her last dwarf rabbit

Dairy cows waiting for the ring at the 2010 Middletown Grange Fair, Wrightstown, Pennsylvania.

named Jack. Soon, my brother was on to bigger animals. He moved from rabbits to pigs and finally settled on dairy cows—Holsteins.

The large livestock pavilion at the fair is the most familiar to me. When I walked into the Bucks County Holstein barn, I first saw a little calf sleeping under a sign stating, "Calf Raffle." I thought, "I wonder what my husband would think if I won a calf." I pictured my husband's shocked face, and the poor little calf sitting in the middle of our postage-stamp yard. I chuckled, but the thought of my brother laughing his ass off made the whole tableau bittersweet. I fought the urge to walk around the Holsteins and try to find Morning Glory Holsteins, to spot my brother's smiling face.

However, he was what led me back to Middletown to walk among the pretty girls. Heifers have glorious dark eyes shrouded by amazing eyelashes. Their necks are silky and shiny, with rolling wrinkles that beckon me to touch them. My hand moved toward a heifer's dehorned head but was stopped by a wet, sniffing nose.

The dairy barn was a hub of activity preparing for the Holstein show. Most of the heifers were washed the night before, but a few stood in the racks getting scrubbed, rinsed and dried. The barn buzzed from all the clippers trimming any stray hairs. When grooming a dairy cow for judging, the whole body needs to be clipped except the top line, the hair along the back. The top line stands up, sometimes with the help of hairspray, to show off the cow's straight back. I carry a picture of my brother with me, taken at the 1991 fair; Dwayne, dressed in his all-whites, kneeling beside his heifer, applies the finishing trim and lift to the top line. I always look for the straight back first when I watch the dairy judging.

The poop duty crew makes sure the pristine cows sit in clean straw. When at the fair with my brother, I always had poop duty. He handed me the pitchfork soon after I arrived, stating, "Get it as soon as it drops." I never minded this job; I knew the importance of keeping the cows clean, and I did anything my brother asked, even clean up shit.

I shook my head as I remembered all the crazy things I did for my brother, when something caught my attention. There, at the end of the pavilion, a little boy, maybe six, clipped his first calf while a woman watched and instructed him. I leaned against a post in the barn and watched. After the boy finished, a gentleman helped the boy hold on to the harness, and they took the calf for a walk. The calf's head immediately went up, and she tried to move away from the pressure of the rope. The handler and the heifer must get accustomed to walking with a harness, which takes hours of practice. Most handlers practice this maneuver throughout the year, but I could see

The photo the author carries with her of her brother, Dwayne E. Helm, preparing his heifer at the 1991 Middletown Grange Fair.

that this was the boy's first time. He was a little shy, his hold tentative. The heifer took advantage of his light hold by leading them both down the path. However, with some guidance, the boy started to get a handle on the power needed to lead the calf. I never mastered the skill of leading a heifer into the show ring, but I remembered being amazed by the power of the animal I held with such a little cord. To feel the heifer's soft hair brush against my knuckle as I put the death grip on the rope, knowing my brother would kill me if I let her get away. I never led a cow into the judging ring, but I was always the extra person to hold the lead when necessary, before or after judging, or to take the heifer to the washroom. I wasn't the leader, my brother was, but I was never too far behind.

Pieces of Me

Doylestown

By Tracy Berthin

I was eighteen when I left Southeastern Pennsylvania for college in another part of the state. Like most young adults, I was happy to go—eager to set out on my own and get away from my hometown and the simple-minded people I'd grown tired of. My family had lived and worked in and died on Bucks and Montgomery County soil for generations. In fact, if we hadn't been peace-loving Mennonite folk, I might even have been entitled to official membership in the Daughters of the American Revolution Club. But no such honor for me. I'm just a plain Jane—of Quaker heritage on my mom's side, although she was raised Presbyterian and doesn't seem to know a lick about the Quakers, and Mennonite heritage on my dad's side, even if he never even attended church, as far as I know. Now, some out-of-town folks assume that since I grew up outside Quakertown, Pennsylvania, I can tell them all about the Quakers. Other innocent inquirers assume that since I mostly grew up attending Mennonite churches, my horse and buggy are parked out back. I just nod, don my bonnet and ask them if they would like some scrapple and shoofly pie later down at the farm. They smile, but it's clear they have no idea what I'm talking about.

So I moved out. I was independent, on my way to finding my place in this world. I was going to do it all. I didn't go far. The next thing I knew, I was married to a Canadian boy and living in upstate New York, only a few hours north of my home state. I'm teaching my kids that Albany is their state's capital and the Erie Canal is a significant local landmark. But the truth is, I'm displaced. Now that I'm raising my own kids out of state, I realize that maybe my Pennsylvania family roots go deeper than I ever considered.

Raising kids is interesting. I find I no longer value as highly the personal independence I did when I left home at eighteen. Though finding one's own identity separate from family is a legitimate journey for every person to take, I feel like I'm coming full circle. Now that I'm raising my four children, some part of me wants to reach back and pull up for them a sense of place, of belonging. I want them to know the people and places they came from so they can somehow appreciate who they are and how they came to be. In order to accomplish this feat, I have had to rediscover my roots.

After getting married, I did live in Pennsylvania for two years in my grandparents' home. I couldn't get any closer to my maternal roots than living in that place. The Brinker—mom's maiden name—homestead was behind our lot, and in the tradition of many farm families, each son was given one acre of land on the property's edge. As my grandfather was one of seven, four of them boys, he got a plot where he built his home between two of his brothers. My grandparents raised my mom and her brother there. Pop Pop was a butcher, with his slaughterhouse and shop out back. When my husband and I lived there, the old meat hooks on pulleys provided a sort of museum and a grand playground for curious guests and their children.

The Brinker homestead as it looked in 1934, when the author's great-grandparents lived there. The farmland was sold, but this home still stands in the middle of the housing development on Brinker Drive (off Lower State Road) in Doylestown.

I learned a lot about my grandparents during those brief years and about their lives in that place. As it turns out, the Brinker name meant something at one time in Doylestown, which was a lot smaller then.

While living there, my dog, Bear, a stray we rescued from the Bensalem Humane Society and a master escape artist, spent many a day roaming the neighborhood wreaking havoc. Chasing him through the yards and open garages of everyone on our street was an interesting way to meet the neighbors. One day, he went missing. I got a call from the local police. Someone had caught him; he was busted. I was sure we'd incur a fine for irresponsible pet ownership. I waited, nervous about the upcoming encounter. The police car drove into our driveway with Bear sitting in the backseat peering guiltily out the back window. I couldn't deny it: our dog was a criminal. I waited for the officer to bring him out and detail the charges. But instead, he got out of the vehicle, took a thoughtful look around the property and asked, "This is Jim Brinker's old place, isn't it?" I hesitated. Was my deceased grandfather's local fame going to get me off the hook?

"Why, yes, Officer, that's right. I'm his granddaughter." After a jolly exchange, he released Bear and drove off. I was glad to be related to Jim.

Not long after, I was standing in line to vote at the township building when a name chiseled into the side of the building caught my eye. It was James M. Brinker, township supervisor. I saw an old GOP representative handing out political literature, so I thought I'd inquire.

"Excuse me, sir, would you happen to know who James M. Brinker is?"

He replied, "Sure! Old Jim was supervisor when this building was erected. He was quite the character. Why do you ask?"

"I'm his granddaughter," I replied. I felt proud to be related to him.

It was about that time that I was struck with the realization that the busy, uppity Doylestown I knew wasn't the same town my mom grew up in. She told me many stories about growing up there, eating at the ice cream parlor, romping in the barn with her cousins, riding her horse through the back field to her grandmother's house. She claims to have once ridden her horse right into town, only to incur the wrath of her father upon her return. Her father attended the one-room schoolhouse in which her maternal grandmother later lived. My mom attended the Central Bucks High School, now called CB West because the area has developed so much to warrant adding East and South High Schools to the district. The fields and the family farm she remembers are now a high-end housing development. The stone homestead stands in the center of that development on a road called Brinker Drive.

My grandparents once took my family to a Doylestown parade. We sat on the front porch of a friend's house watching the parade go by. My grandfather knew everybody over the age of fifty. Whether it was a fellow Mason, a political crony, a local farmer, an old business associate, a layperson from the church or just a buddy he ate breakfast with at the Cracker Crumb, he knew them all. It's difficult to understand how much the town has changed—how big and busy it is now, how detached the people are from one another. The remnants of the old families who had a hand in building the town are mostly long gone, busy building lives elsewhere.

I'm a Stauffer by name, not a Brinker. When I attended a Stauffer family reunion in 2003, I didn't know anyone there outside my parents and my aunt. We were given a family booklet that held a record of known information about our branch in the Stauffer family tree, which was fascinating to me as I discovered that I come from a long line of Mennonite farmers who first arrived in the land of Penn in 1710, after escaping persecution in Europe for their faith. In this family booklet, every generation is listed as being a Southeastern Pennsylvania farmer and a Mennonite until my grandfather's generation, when he stopped farming and was not a practicing Mennonite. Certainly, my Pennsylvania Mennonite farming history has left a deposit in me in terms of the values and traditions that I hold to, despite the changes in society. Can it be that if I choose not to at least recognize those values and therefore fail to transfer them to the next generation that those two hundred plus years are lost forever, that those lines of people's lives in the booklet are just a distant shadow with no relevance anymore? Perhaps one day in the future this family booklet will be distributed at a reunion, updated with my own name and birth and death dates on it.

Much of my personal history I can only imagine. I have a list of names, dates and places, some photos and random stories. My relatives didn't take much time to instill in me a sense of family heritage. They didn't really tell their stories; I guess they thought they didn't matter. My paternal grandfather, Phares, was one of sixteen kids raised on the family farm. Pop Pop Stauffer had a strong Pennsylvania Dutch accent that was difficult to understand, but he told the same few stories over and over, so we came to know them by heart. He loved to tell the story about the first car they ever saw in the neighborhood, how the owner drove it into the back of the barn yelling, "Whoa! Whoa!" in an attempt to make it stop. Another favorite was the time someone rigged up an electric fence line to the outhouse and literally shocked a visiting relative who thought he'd been stung by a bee. My grandfather became an egg huckster but tried his hand at farming for a brief time while my father was young. My dad, also named Phares, remembers fondly those years on the farm and has revisited the land with his younger sister. My dad has retired to a twenty-seven-acre farmette, where he can play with his tractors in wide-open spaces. My son, Michael Phares, spends a lot of time on those tractors with his Pop Pop.

As I teach my own children early American history, I recognize that my family's roots are tied to the roots of this nation. I'm proud of that fact. Pennsylvania's story is my family's story, for it was people like my ancestors who built the commonwealth. They weren't rich or famous, not founding fathers or Revolutionary soldiers—Mennonites opted not to fight in wars—but they were part of a brave mass of early German immigrants who chose to embrace freedom and build their families, their communities and their livelihoods in a new, independent world. They held to their beliefs, culture and lifestyle for hundreds of years and passed that history to me.

Landscape Design

Oreland

By Laura M. Gibson

The first night my husband John, son Owen and I slept in our new house in Oreland, just north of Philadelphia, I lay awake and sobbed. It was the end of July, sweltering, oppressive. In our small mountain town out West, even our summer nights had been cool and quiet and very dark. I sweated among the sheets and tried to shut my ears against the din—not against the rasp of cicadas and one very industrious owl, but against the constant pulse of traffic that rose above it, as if the beat of so many living in so few square miles was an amplified drumline in the heart of the night.

I got up and went outside and saw that up and down our tree-lined street, so quaint in the daytime, every single property had a bright streetlight. During the day, our Philadelphia suburb felt like a small town with its few businesses and wide, sidewalked streets, but at night, it was an eerie compound pushing against the dark. Above this glow, the lights of Philadelphia cast a greenish hue that skirted a band of high clouds.

Standing on the curb, I considered our choice to come East. Our other life had included as much time in the woods as we could get and still keep our jobs. I liked to get dirty, to sleep outside under a star-pulsing sky and watch for meteor showers, to grow my own food and share it. That night, one thing became clear to me: while I was up for the challenge and opportunity of learning to love a new landscape, I felt I might fail.

The second night, Stuart and his wife, Denice, invited us next door for a cocktail on their patio. We wandered over after a sticky day of unpacking without air conditioning and were ushered into their freezing home, identical in floor plan to our own. We walked through the living room with its white leather couches and brass lighting, its massive TV media center and then past the dining room furniture protected with clear plastic. The house smelled strongly of Lysol and Tilex, and Denice confessed as we made our way to the backyard that she'd just been "down on hands and knees cleaning the kitchen floor by hand."

"You just can't imagine the kinds of bugs I find along those baseboards," she said, smiling. She had dark hair and large brown—almost black—eyes; she talked using her manicured hands for emphasis. "It makes my skin crawl." She put her hands behind her and arched her lower back; I saw that she was pregnant, which seemed like a good sign. There'd be a child for our son Owen to play with.

On the patio in their backyard, we sat and drank wine as Owen, who was two, amused himself trying to climb a small dogwood. Twilight fell as we got to know one another. Stuart was an accountant who worked two towns over. Denice was a geriatric nurse at a local community hospital. The lusty SOS of fireflies rose up into the trees; the shrill of cicadas and the moist, heavy air seemed exotic.

"I'm getting ready to do some landscaping," Stuart said, vaguely waving in the direction of his backyard. I looked out over his domain with him. A utility shed shaped like a barn sat toward the back of the property. The shed's doors were open and revealed a collection of tools: a lawnmower and leaf-blowing system, bags of fertilizer, several outdoor toys for their future child.

"He stays so busy in this big yard," Denice said. "It's just *so* not my thing."

Stuart's backyard, like ours, was a large, flat quarter acre with a hillside at the back that rose to the golf course our properties abutted. But where our whole yard, including the hillside, was rimmed with overgrown trees and shrubs taller than our house, Stuart and Denice's yard had a linear, bald symmetry to it. Their hillside was covered in pachysandras and three pruned rhododendrons. On either side of the yard were a series of small privacy shrubs—forsythia, more rhododendron, hibiscus—and closest to our yard was a stand of three gorgeous hemlocks that provided shade from the afternoon sun on that side of the yard. I imagined Stuart had big plans in this clean-slated space. I was curious to see how his inspiration would take shape.

In the weeks afterward, I watched as Stuart had the perimeter of his house sprayed with pesticides to keep out the spiders, stink bugs, millipedes and bees. A lawn company rolled its truck to the curb and shot liquid fertilizer out of a hose so that his grass would turn an emerald green. A security company alarm-wired the windows. The little dogwood in their backyard came down. One morning, I saw that the shrubbery that had flanked one side of the backyard was resting in the gutter, waiting for the trash truck. Each time we spoke about his landscape "plan," which seemed to involve nothing besides razing his property, Stuart talked about how he'd taken action because he was afraid something would happen. "This way," he said, "I don't have to worry about it."

I understood the impulse to want to shape one's space. After all, on my own land I was doing the same—I'd put in a native plant bed in the front yard, a raised bed for veggies in the backyard. John and I had finished off a section of fencing so that our dogs could roam free in the backyard while we were at work. On the top of the forested hillside out back, I waged a series of battles with the ivy choking several oak trees. So, I was busy taming my landscape, too. What I had a hard time understanding was the way fear seemed to be the bedrock of Stuart's "landscaping."

The day he removed the hemlocks, which were just outside our bedroom window and were also the home to a family of wrens we could hear merrily chatting every morning, I was so angry I could hardly speak. I stayed indoors, played my music too loudly and angrily cleaned the house while I thought of ways to sabotage Stuart's gardening life. By the time I went outside, I still felt a little reckless; part of me hoped something Stuart said would set me off. I stood in the front yard with him and watched the crew climb the second tree to limb it. Although it was fully fall, Stuart wore his standard gardening clothes—a pair of red shorts, a gray Philadelphia Eagles T-shirt torn near his right shoulder and white tennis shoes.

"How will your child learn to climb trees, Stuart?"

He shook his head without looking at me. "I've been meaning to do this since I bought the place," he said. "Good riddance." He blew on his hands and rubbed them together.

"But they're fantastic," I said. "They keep that part of the house shady and cool in summer, I bet."

He shrugged. "We have great air conditioning."

"Did you know trees are good for us? Remember biology?"

"I guess," he shrugged. "But I'm worried they'll fall on the house."

"They must be older than the house," I said. "Think of what you've done."

"Old and in the way," he said. He looked at me. "You're mad," he said.

I thought of the big ash trees in our old front yard and the way they shielded us against the afternoon light; I thought of our new front yard with its giant oak tree—it surely was twice as old as the house—and how we were going to put in a rope swing for Owen from its lowermost branch. Across the street, our neighbor Meredith still had a stand of hemlocks. She'd placed a garden bench underneath, which she often sat in for a few minutes, watching the clothes she'd hung out on the line flutter in the breeze. I wanted to shout at Stuart, to yank the arborist out of the tree by the tail of his harness rope.

"Yes. I'm mad. What'll you plant instead?" I asked.

"Probably nothing," he said. "I got this baby coming. We're almost ready."

The crew began their work on the last tree. Stuart opened a Diet Pepsi he'd stored in his back pocket and took a long drink. The blinds in the dining room opened, and Denice gave him a thumbs up, which Stuart returned. She waved at me, smiling, and then closed the blinds.

When the crew left, the place where the hemlocks had been was a naked nub of earth.

"You know," he said before he turned to go inside, "if you cut down your trees, we wouldn't have so many leaves to pick up."

"Not a chance," I said.

"I know," he said.

And so it began, our landscape war. I had no intention of yielding and making his yard work easier, of course, but I began to pay closer attention to his wish to make it so. His son, Regan, a baby with colic, was born in early November of that year, and Denice was having a pretty serious case of postpartum depression. Stuart worked long hours. He'd come straight home and help out with the baby. He worked hard in his yard, doing all the work himself, sometimes out there after dark with a headlamp on. On a few occasions, I caught him leaning against a fencepost after dark, his headlamp turned off, shoulders slumped, watching the windows of his own house. Even with the windows closed, we could hear the baby wailing inside.

Often, he'd come out when he saw John or I, or both of us, outside. I came to understand that Stuart was jealous of the way John and I worked together in our landscape. Often on Friday nights, our version of a cheap date was to follow mowing and weeding with pizza and beer. Denice disliked most seasons, either because of the bugs, the extreme temperature or the rain; Stuart was always in his yard alone. I imagined life inside his house was lonely, too.

Still, the pesticides, the general zeal for chemicals, the noise pollution, the obsession with preparedness—these were more than distressing to me. Stuart seemed to have no idea the harm he was exposing his family to in the name of safety, not to mention the way his vigilance infringed on the way others might wish to live. Our yard was slightly downhill from his; when it rained, runoff from his yard came into ours and then moved down the street. When he sprayed for bugs, those chemicals leached into the air, the soil, the groundwater. And though Stuart navigated in the world as if he were his own spaceship, I couldn't believe he didn't see that he was infecting our shared world. Running underneath "preemptive" were ignorance and fear, it seemed to me, qualities that weren't particular to Stuart's house. They were writ much larger in the world.

Most weekends, Stuart got out his leaf blower and vacuumed his yard. Most weekends, he offered to loan the device to me. In the beginning, his insistence that I use his tools made me angry, especially since I'd made a point to tell him I enjoyed the bone-tired ache a day in the yard could deliver. One day, I saw him cock his head and smile, then hold out his leaf blower to me with both hands. "Seriously," he said. "It'd be so easy."

"It feels like a drug deal," I said. I leaned on my rake, considering how I'd missed that Stuart might've been teasing me for longer than I'd noticed.

"But it sucks *and* blows," he said.

"You sound like an infomercial," I said. "Try raking. It's quiet."

"I like racket," he said. "Then I don't hear the voices in my head. I think you might be a hippie."

"Peace, love and no leaf blowers, man," I said.

This banter became a kind of ritual that peppered our outdoor work. Looking back, the memory of our gardening relationship is one of the sharpest from my time in Pennsylvania: the bourbon-hued leaves blanketing both our yards, the sound of the rake resisting the leaf blower, the camaraderie of Stuart's parallel work, the way—just before we moved—he told me my organic ways had given him a lot to think about.

He mowed and bagged, or blew leaves into piles or squirted fertilizer onto the grass out of a tankard strapped to his back, and then our conversation would pick up where we'd left off.

"You know you could compost those clippings if you didn't use pesticides," I'd say.

He'd wave his leaf blower at me. I'd brandish my rake.

"Really? You don't want to cut down that oak tree in the front yard?" he'd say.

"Not a chance," I'd say.

The second autumn I lived in the neighborhood, fear came to visit all of us. September 11 and the anthrax attacks happened just one week apart. Like many, I felt it was hard to reconcile the jigsaw of despair and anger, kindness and hope. The new age of hateful patriotism was frightening, rendering us even more ill-equipped to deal with a world that had, it seemed, gone mad. I spent more time hiking in a piece of forest I loved. I baked dozens of loaves of bread and recall many nights reading by the fire with Owen. I stopped watching television.

At the end of that September, Stuart and I were in the yard dealing with the leaves. Denice opened her dining room window to lament that Regan had been up all night with an ear infection. After a little while, Stuart turned his leaf blower off and walked over to where I was cutting back a butterfly bush.

"You ever read *The Stand* by Stephen King?" he said. We stood in the side yard, near the place where the hemlocks had been.

I put a fistful of clippings into the wheelbarrow and took my gloves off. He went on to tell me King was a genius. That here it was. Captain Tripps. In real life.

"Remember that disease that killed off most of the world?" he said. He looked a little walleyed, standing there in his torn gardening shirt, the nozzle of his leaf blower dragging on the ground like a club. "Come on," he said. "I want to show you my anthrax room."

"Your what?"

"Just come on," he said.

We went inside his house and walked past the television tuned to a daytime show. The pumpkin-sized head of an unnaturally tan actor who was crying filled the screen. "Denice's damned DVR-ed soaps," Stuart called over his shoulder to me. I heard the baby crying behind his closed bedroom door and Denice shushing him. We made our way down the hallway to the bedroom at the end of it. In both our houses, this room was a guest room and office. Stuart had turned this space into an anthrax room. I scanned the space—a refrigerator, a desk with a computer and chair. On one wall he'd assembled two sets of metal and particle-board bookshelves on which sat his supplies: a hotplate, his computer, a supply of canned goods, silverware and dishes, several gallons of water, plastic and duct tape to cover the windows, a supply of diapers and stacks of pillows and blankets. A portable toilet was stashed next to the closet.

I refrained from saying that my anthrax room would have beer, chocolate and books. Stuart seemed eager for me to approve. Warm air from a heating vent above my head kicked on.

"Stuart, how did you come up with this idea?" I asked.

"There was this great piece on the local news," he said. "Check this out." He lifted up the phone receiver and listened. "I even have a separate phone line."

"I'm not sure we're the kinds of people targeted by anthrax," I said.

He scratched his belly for a moment, and I noticed the rip in the shirt had gotten larger. "But we could be," he said. "Trace amounts from one letter can touch another in the mail, and then...you know."

"I just don't think this is how it's going to end," I said.

"But I worry," he said.

"Don't you miss having the office space?"

I wondered then if Stuart's nightmares were not all that different from his waking fears: someone might break in and steal his son, a tree might fall on his house, intruders might mess with his yard in the night, traveling to other countries might get him kidnapped, or sick or lead to his identity being stolen. I went home shaking my head that day, feeling I'd failed in telling Stuart that his idea was cracked. Part of me wondered whether I was the crazy one for not preparing my own family for pending disaster, whether there was wisdom and safety to be found in Stuart's brand of disconnect.

A few weeks later, I spoke with him again. There had been more anthrax letter scares in the news but not yet the plague Stuart feared. We were in the front yard, where he was waving the wand of his backpack blower vac, trying to suck leaves out of the fall wind. He saw me walking toward him and turned the motor off.

"So," I said. "How's it going?"

"Actually," he avoided making eye contact, "I'm kind of embarrassed. It seemed like such a good idea."

For a minute, I felt a little trill, thinking he was talking about his leaf blower. He nodded his head in the direction of his house. "Ah. The room," I said. "These are scary times."

"I guess. I think I might take it down. It's just. You want to be safe in the world, you know?"

I nodded, wondering if we were doomed as a species. How would we ever survive if we were capable of the kinds of acts we'd experienced that September? "Maybe the best any of us can hope for is to do a good job with our own families."

"Hey, you know you can borrow my leaf blower," he said half-heartedly.

"I know," I said and took my rake to the backyard.

In 2004, John and I had another child, a daughter named Riley. Denice was pregnant with their second child, and Regan, at three years old, was a handful. He liked to help me rake on the weekends, much to Stuart's dismay.

One day that October, I raked leaves in the front yard while Riley sat on a blanket at the base of the oak tree playing with blocks. On the heels of such a devastating set of years, led by an administration that seemed to have bungled just about every aspect of governing and yet had the audacity to be smug about its insistence that fear drive the country's collective rage, I felt it wasn't enough just to vote. For several weeks, Riley and I had been beating the pavement, and I was very far out of my comfort zone proselytizing to neighbors I hardly knew. Again and again MoveOn requested me to visit homes where people were undecided, to revisit those who'd made up their minds, to organize rides to polls for people. The work was intense at times; the neighbors were tired of answering their doors. I wasn't sure the neighborhood canvass model was really working.

A fire engine lumbered by and parked down the street followed by a news van. They quieted their engines and got out of their vehicles. Pretending not to notice the entourage as it approached me walking in a clutched group down the middle of the street, I continued raking. An attractive blond newscaster and her train of five—one camerawoman and four firemen in their dress uniforms from our township—strolled into my driveway. They were all grinning at me, each craning a neck to meet my eyes. I recognized the strategy. It was one I was using myself to canvass. I felt uncomfortable at the spear end of someone else's efforts.

The group stopped at the end of the drive, and the newscaster called me over. We stood behind my car a few feet apart. It was early, about eight thirty in the morning; the last school bus had just barreled past on its way back to the bus barn. Our mornings, after we took Owen to first grade, were not very structured. We were not expecting visitors. I reached around behind me to discover that the hem of my flannel nightgown was hanging out of my sweatpants and below my sweatshirt. Despite the ripped baseball cap, which covered my hair pulled back into a ponytail, what protruded was a mess, I was sure of it.

The blonde wore a red blazer and extended her hand.

"Hi," she sounded southern, "I'm Susan Callahan with Channel Six news. How are you today?" Her head was cocked to one side. I shook her hand. Her red lipstick was thick and bright, some of it smudged on her front teeth. I had assumed she was on our street to do some canvassing of her own. Our county, Montgomery, was a battleground in the national campaign—for months we'd been inspected by the media through a searing political lens. Despite my attire, general abhorrence of being on camera and certainty that whatever I was about to say probably wouldn't be all that articulate, I timidly looked forward to a lively political debate, back-framed by my pajamas and telling bumper sticker slogans: *Defend America. Defeat Bush. Smart Women Vote. Think: It's Patriotic.* I was willing to be on television, even the local news, to talk about politics.

She dropped my hand and opened her slim leather binder. Her companions waited behind her. One of them wandered over and knelt down next to Riley, who held out one drool-covered alphabet block to him.

"I was wondering if you knew that it's Fire Prevention Week?" Susan asked. An adolescent lilt rang at the end of her question. "Have you checked to see that your smoke detectors are working?"

I wondered if I heard her correctly. It was four days before perhaps the most important presidential election in both of our lifetimes, and she wasn't going to talk about it. I leaned on my rake again.

"I'm happy to chat, but I don't want to be on TV," I said. The camerawoman said, "Oops," from behind her lens but didn't put her camera down or turn it off. I tugged at the brim of my baseball cap.

"Oh. Well. You wouldn't want to answer a few questions for us, then?" The record light on the camera was still blinking.

Susan Callahan continued talking. She wanted to come into my house and film my functioning smoke detectors to show people what a prepared-for-fire citizen looked like. No doubt they'd walk behind me, filming the inside of my house and the tail of my flannel pajamas before we'd stop at the

House in Oreland.

detector and determine, "Yep. It's working. Look at the little blinky light." She wanted me to stand next to one of my township firemen for a photo op so I could be in the local paper.

"We just really want people to think about danger," she said.

I bit the inside of my cheek. It was a small thing to be a good sport, to participate in the safekeeping of my community in this way. I thought about the anthrax room, about the way the oversized televisions in my neighborhood, which we could see through windows when we walked the streets with our dogs at night, created a collective flickering glow all around us. How this odd ritual of participating in the world actually unmoored us from one another in the way that Orwell depicted so well. Encouraged us to do such a thing as build an anthrax room. To practice intolerance of our neighbors. To be afraid.

"I'd really rather not," I said. I took a step back toward the lawn.

There was a pregnant, disbelieving pause. I could see they were perplexed by someone who did not want to be on TV. Susan thanked me and turned to leave, followed by the camera and the firemen.

"Hey, Susan!" I called. "I know someone who might want to chat with you." Her face lit up, and she opened her leather folder again.

I sent them next door to Stuart's house. He opened the door and looked past them toward where I stood in our joint side yard. I brandished my rake in his direction. He smiled and shook his head, then invited them in.

Reconstructing Germantown

Germantown

By Carrie Hagen

On the surface, suburban white kids seem pretty similar. I know the games have changed since I grew up, but when I visit my parents in Levittown today, I still see boys and girls chasing one another on their bikes and hear them arguing over street hockey rules. Like my brothers and I did, they walk down the block to school, and when summer finally arrives, it will bring camps, mid-week sleepovers and new nets on the public basketball courts. I don't remember much about those schools at the end of the block, but I do remember walking back and forth with the neighborhood kids. I also remember some of our talks. If I hid behind the bushes on Old Mr. Richardson's property, I'm sure I'd hear some of the same conversations today: banter about teachers, frenemies, the ethnic guessing game and the urban challenge.

The ethnic guessing game allowed us to assert our identities while evaluating our similarities—though of course we didn't understand this psychology then. Somebody would begin by asking somebody else about her heritage. "Are you Italian? You look Russian. Are you Chinese or are you Japanese?" The conversation kept going until everyone in the group identified their roots. When it was my turn, I proudly identified myself as "Welsh, Scottish and Irish." Years after my grandfather died, Dad learned that Granddad had lied about his pure Irish blood. "He was more German than anything, " Dad said. "He just didn't like it."

The urban challenge was more competitive. It was a way for someone to earn "street cred" by proving he or she had a closer connection to the inner city than anyone else. Everyone wanted to participate, but not everyone could. Those who had no urban ties bowed out after mumbling the name of a cousin's fake boyfriend from South Philly or a camp friend from Kensington. Luckily for me, I had an inside edge on this rivalry. I never had to lie. After hearing a few claims, I could say, "My dad grew up in Germantown." Some may have had a parent born in the Northeast or Center City, but few had a dad from an African American neighborhood known for crime and vandalism. The others could only nod and look away. Point for potential street smarts: me.

I wouldn't have admitted it five years ago, but when I started writing *we is got him*, a narrative true-crime story set in Germantown, I was trying to insert myself into my father's stomping grounds. I lived in Philadelphia by then, having settled in the young professional Art Museum section a few neighborhoods southeast of Germantown. The move brought me closer to urbanite status, but I had chosen the path of the metropolitan bourgeoisie, not that of the savvy urban cowboy I had so wanted the other kids to admire.

— • —

The Philadelphia in *we is got him* exists in 1870s Victorian America, but what drew me to it was the Germantown that hosted my father's stories from the 1950s and '60s. Dad would take my brothers and me to visit that world occasionally on a Sunday afternoon. It looked different from what he had described. Without knowing how to say it, we could tell that history had eroded whatever had put the twinkle in his eye. He didn't care how run-down a block had become—and the potholes only got bigger over the years—he saw Germantown as it existed in his adolescence, and after hearing enough stories, so did we. From our back seats in the beige Dodge Caravan, my brothers and I asked Dad to repeat particular stories year after year. The more we knew them, the more important the order of his storytelling became. If he left something out—or worse, left it out and didn't remember its being there in the first place—we needed him to confirm our memories. I think we were afraid that if he didn't validate them, we would somehow change.

Our trips tended to follow a particular path. They started at Dad's earliest home and traced the moves his family of six made until he enlisted in the army. I remember the house on Upsal Street, across from the shell of a Baptist church, where Uncle Terry shimmied up a light post and fell off, and the place on Chew Street, where they stayed until the landlord put up a For Sale sign without telling them. The home I liked hearing about most was an apartment in "The Ship," a former World War II brothel frequented by navy boys on leave. The Ship was near the edge of "The Brickyard"—a few blocks named for the Irish bricklayers who had once lived there. Granddad had grown up there, too. He was a member of the original Brickyard Gang, local low-income boys who protected the neighborhood from the Red Spots, a gang from Nicetown who wore marks to resemble blood on their white T-shirts. When the Red Spots ventured too far north, the groups brawled in the quarry with slingshots and BB guns. Granddad liked to fight. He came from a long line of bricklayers and mill or factory workers in Philadelphia. Even with his two full-time jobs—laboring at a steel factory during the day and driving a truck at night—he couldn't pay the bills. To avoid the bill collectors who would show up unannounced at the front door, the family moved from one block to another.

◄─────►

Many years later, I would learn about the first families who moved to Germantown. They were Germans who fled from religious persecution to William Penn's offer of religious asylum in 1683. They lived in caves, log cabins and sod huts as they established a village on either side of an uphill Indian trail. At first dependent on Philadelphia's loans, the community of craftsmen and artisans developed a reputation for their meticulous handiwork and used their earnings to declare financial independence before neighboring settlements could. Over the next two hundred years, the trail that ran through Germantown became a national historic landmark. Quakers and Mennonites met along it in 1688 to sign the nation's first protest against slavery. General Washington's men marched down it in shame in 1777, after they lost the hard-fought Battle of Germantown. By the 1860s, slaves had crept over it on their way to the Johnson House, Philadelphia's only documented stop on the Underground Railroad.

The trail, which changed from a road to a street to an avenue, was horrible to travel. Horses, settlers, soldiers and wagon wheels tripped and dodged the rocks, puddles, divots and broken cobblestone that lined the

"Quaint Old Germantown in Pennsylvania," four of a series of sixty former landmarks of Germantown and vicinity drawn on zinc during the years 1863–88, by John Richards. *Courtesy La Salle University's Connolly Library.*

Illustration from Christian K. Ross's *Charley Ross, the Kidnapped Child. The Father's Story* (Philadelphia: John E. Potter and Company, 1876).

thoroughfare. Yet on either side, the village blossomed into a beautiful suburb and then a city neighborhood. Throughout these years, wealthy immigrants had their native flowers shipped to estates that already benefitted from a wide breadth of flora and fauna. To the east and west of the avenue in 1874, oak, chestnut, walnut and locust trees lined the streets. Around the creeks and streams scattered in the valleys, wildflowers sprung around blackberry bushes and ferns. Peddlers traveled through this idyllic setting, selling their wares at the front doors of Colonial houses, Victorian mansions and Gothic cottages. On a July day in 1874, two of them stole two little boys from their father's front yard. They let one go, but not the other, setting off a flawed investigation that failed to solve the first ransom kidnapping in American history.

The case would symbolize America's growing pains as it moved between its first and second centuries. To reclaim its identity from a divisive war and an industrial push that bankrupted craftsmen, America invited the world to a centennial celebration. The government hoped that a decorative display of progress would unite the country and assure the world that the Civil War had not weakened American resolve. Philadelphia, Congress decided, would host the party. Three days after the kidnappers took Charley Ross, the mayor broke ground on the centennial site. Over the next two years, the Charley Ross case would test the young police forces in Philadelphia and New York, call attention to the exploitation of children as Victorian objects in the workplace and the home and disappear from the front pages of the newspapers as centennial excitement captured the city.

⟶•⟵

Dad grew up in Germantown over seventy years after Charley disappeared. It was his story that I had first wanted to write, his narrative that led me to Charley's.

I decided to write about Germantown when I entered an MFA program and needed a focus for a nonfiction manuscript. I felt a connection to Germantown, to the stories along the avenue, where so many families like mine had traveled up and down, east to west. Maybe it was residue from my perceived bragging rights as a child, but I felt as if something existed in that part of the city that belonged to me. Perhaps in trying to write my father's memoir, I thought re-creating his stories would make them my own.

It was easy to reconstruct the physical landscape of family stories. The Sunday afternoon minivan drives had given me a keen sense of geography, and interviews with family and community members reinforced the image of Germantown that I had come to romanticize: the ball fields where Dad became a sports star; the all-American-looking high school across from the enlisting post at town hall; the fences behind the row homes where women gathered while they waited for laundry to dry outside. Peddlers walked down the back alleys between these fences. Women and children recognized their voices before their calls; they knew the pitches of the scissor-sharpening man, the umbrella man, the strawberry and fresh tomato sellers, the clothing man.

But these memories were someone else's recollections, pieces of a larger story that I desperately wanted to tell. The problem was that I didn't know what it was about. I loved the setting, and I loved the characters, but I had scenes without a theme. I thought that perhaps integrating a social issue would focus the project. Dad and his friends grew up during the first waves of the mid-twentieth century's "white flight" to the suburbs, and I knew that the neighborhood was undergoing gentrification as young white individuals and families took advantage of its affordably spacious, historic housing. I returned to the stories that I had, reaching out to new contacts with the hope that I could find a narrative that reconciled Germantown's proud history of diversity with the exodus of white families in the twentieth century and the struggles of gentrification in the twenty-first.

As good as the topic sounded, and as much as I clung to the Sunday stories that I loved, I struggled to identify the scope of my research. Surrounded by textbooks of social history, I realized I had no understanding of the politics

73

of my topic. To know it was to live it. If this were the story that I wanted to write, I needed to move to Germantown. I needed to leave the safer confines of my neighborhood and become the research topic. I was, after all, a child of someone who had moved from Germantown to Levittown. I was now reentering that landscape, interested in its history and its gentrification. The story wasn't really my father's. It was mine. And that was when I realized that I couldn't really tell it.

Liberal politics aside, part of me has always known that no matter how much I want to identify with Germantown's people, I can never be one of them. Not necessarily because of racial or economic differences, nor because its working-class locals and bohemian transplants wouldn't welcome a new neighbor. I can't be one of them because I don't want to live with them, really. I want to live with the ghosts that live in their houses, the figments of my father's romantic imagination, a world that doesn't exist. A fiction.

So I decided to dig a little further into the past, where I found a nineteenth-century world full of people I didn't know. I could tell Charley's story, and I could reconstruct his landscape, because I had no part in it and no expectations for it.

Still, *we is got him* has allowed me to write about Germantown, to package it and put my name on it. And in that way, I suppose I am one of the characters from its history book. Not the boy on the ball field, or the soldier on the avenue or the Irish bricklayer returning home to The Ship. But their ghosts might sense me, walking down the streets, hoping someone will hear my voice and come to see what I have to sell.

Flow

Philadelphia
By Lori Litchman

The Schuylkill River is a vast sewer system. From this sewer comes the drinking water which supplies a large proportion of the one million inhabitants of Philadelphia.
—Philadelphia Inquirer, *July 25, 1889*

I drink from the Schuylkill River daily. Not directly, of course. But all of the water the city pipes into my home for the small fee of thirty-five dollars a month comes from the Schuylkill. I also know that because of Philadelphia's outdated underground water and sewer system—which consists of creeks buried in sewage pipes—every time it rains, raw sewage enters the Schuylkill. But despite knowing what I know about the health of the water in the river, I decided that traveling outside the city and then kayaking into Philadelphia— rather than driving, biking or walking in—might be the way for me to spice up my relationship with Philly. We'd been going through a sort of fifteen-year itch. I figured the freedom of the open river would help me see my love from a new perspective, at which point I would magically feel all of those old feelings and fall back in love with my adopted urban metropolis. I pictured myself effortlessly paddling into the city guided by a gentle breeze, water lightly lapping against my kayak, sun sneaking though the trees along the shore, casting rays of soft light onto the crystal-clear water, as I saw the city from a different perspective, one where I immediately realized how much I love this urban paradise of Philadelphia. I knew this trip would change my relationship with the city forever.

I couldn't have been more wrong.

I had purchased a kayak the previous fall, certain I would be out on the water every week. After one trip through a particularly polluted creek, my boat sat parked for months. I decided that my first real trip should be a journey of 110 miles down the Schuylkill River with about 150 other people, ending in Philadelphia. The annual Schuylkill River Sojourn is a time for outdoor enthusiasts to take to the river to enjoy a few days of kayaking with like-minded folks and to call attention to the health of the river. At this point in my life, my doctor had advised me to lose about forty pounds from my petite five-foot-one frame and to start exercising more. I thought this trip would be a good way to start my health kick.

My kayaking trip started in Schuylkill Haven, a two-hour drive and a metaphorical world away from Philadelphia. The air was clean and smelled of dew and trees, the roads were narrow and the buildings were nearly all residential. It reminded me a lot of Northeastern Pennsylvania, where I grew up.

After a good night's sleep, I awoke at dawn on Saturday morning, eager to get on the water. A heavy fog blanketed the river, making the lush green trees—river birch, maples, catalpas—only shadows. A picture of me at the boat launch shows me smiling as I embarked on my journey. I'm sure I wasn't sweating at this point, and the hat that didn't leave my head for the vast

The author (center) sets off on her journey. *Photo by Dave Tavani.*

majority of the endeavor hadn't found its way on yet. The first day's journey was only fifteen and a half miles of paddling. When I pushed off, I yelled to my husband, Dave, "See you in Philadelphia!" The morning remained cool and misty for the first hour. Perfectly formed spider webs glistened as a two-mile brigade of boats drifted by. We passed old stone bridges lined with cheering onlookers. I had never participated in any sport where people stood and cheered. It felt great to see so many people showing their support. So far, it was everything I had hoped the trip would be.

But then it started getting hot. Really hot. The beginning of a weeklong, over-ninety-degree-heat-wave hot. And as I clumsily dodged rocks, I began getting wet. And my arms started to really hurt. I found out several hours into the trip that I had been holding my paddle upside down and not using my torso correctly. The proper way to paddle is to use the midsection as a pivot, relying mostly on abdominal muscles to propel the boat forward. I had been using only my arms while holding my paddle incorrectly. By lunchtime the first day, the picture of me changed dramatically. I don't remember what I ate for lunch, but I do remember it didn't take me very long to eat and that I was first in line for medical attention. Now donning my sun hat, a picture shows me stretched out on the ground before our wilderness first aid guide, "Dr. Matt," as he patched up the many blisters I'd managed to get on both of my wet heels.

After lunch, I felt a little better and figured I could handle the rest of the day's journey. But then, we hit flat, placid water, and I suddenly felt like I was paddling through a morass of mud. And then came the sign I most dreaded to see during the trip: "Danger Dam! Portage Here." This sign meant that I had to get out of my boat and carry it—all forty pounds of it—around the Auburn Dam, the first of eight dams throughout the entire trip.

Dams are to rivers what clots are to hearts. By controlling the ebb and flow of the water, dams essentially alter the river's hydrology—or the river's circulatory system. The flow of the river is forever reduced downstream of the dam, affecting the river's flora and fauna. Damming rivers causes riverbank erosion, which leads to the domination of invasive species along the riparian buffer or bank. The dams also prevent anadromous fish such as shad from being able to swim upstream to reproduce. Many municipalities across the country, now aware of damming's devastating effects, are spending millions of dollars to either tear down dams or build fish ladders to propel fish upstream through the dam without causing them any harm. As I carried my boat, with help from one of my fellow paddlers, I cursed the dam and wondered if any radical environmental groups would be interested in blowing it up. I made a mental note to investigate this possibility if I made it out of my journey alive.

When I got to the flag marking the end of the day's journey, I almost started to cry out of both joy and pain. Two strapping gents—or maybe they were skinny retirees—pulled my boat out of the water. I remember one of them saying I looked weary, which didn't come close to describing how I felt. I was near death. I pitched my tent like a bird with a broken wing, fighting the pain in my arms every time I attempted to move them. I couldn't wait to lie down and sleep. Along with my fellow hundred or so kayakers, I walked to the local fire hall for the spaghetti dinner graciously provided for us, gobbled it down and then walked slowly back to camp. It took all the energy I could muster to zip open my tent, after which I crawled inside and crashed. Except, I couldn't fall asleep. I'm borderline narcoleptic and can sleep through anything—including a murder on my block, which consisted of gunshots and sirens. I tried to lie motionless to stem the flow of pain. I took two extra-strength pain pills and, even though I'm an atheist, thought about praying for the pain to go away. Muscles I didn't even know I had hurt. I somehow managed to doze off for a couple hours, when the sounds of roosters crowing invaded my restless sleep. It was only 4:00 a.m., and the roosters wouldn't quit. Though I didn't think it possible, I hurt more than when I had dozed off. Not only was I sore, but my muscles had also stiffened as no thirty-three-year-old's should. I cursed the chickens and wished them dead. The chickens stopped about 6:00 a.m., right around the time the train went by blowing its whistle. Our resting area, Port Clinton, a well-known train town, was a major stop on the Reading and Pennsylvania lines during the railroad's heyday.

I was miserable. One day down, six days and ninety-six miles to go. I loaded up my gear, chased more than the recommended amount of pain medicine with a cup of bad coffee and set out on day two.

I really didn't think I was going to make it. But I couldn't give in just yet. I put my boat in the water and got through it one paddle at a time. Though I don't remember much, a picture shows me smiling as I bounce through some currents and swoosh around a rock and paddle, paddle, paddle to prevent my boat from capsizing. Most of the day I spent counting strokes with my paddle, just to take my mind off the aches. I forced myself to paddle ten times, then twenty and thirty before I took a break. When I packed in the morning, something had told me to take my cellphone with me in my dry bag in my boat. At lunch, I called Dave and asked him to come pick me up at the end of the day's paddle. I was throwing in the towel. I was done. Thirty-four miles down, zero to go. I was a quitter. The rest of the day's paddle went by a bit easier since I knew there was a way out at the end of the day.

When we arrived at our stopping point for the day—Jim Dietrich Park in Montgomery County—I parked my boat and got in the dinner line. I wolfed down a veggie burger and some Coke and waited for my carriage to arrive. When Dave got there, I hugged him as best I could given my condition and burst out with, "What the hell was I thinking?" He smiled and shrugged. "I didn't want to discourage you," he said. We sat and chatted for a while, and I told him that I really didn't want to give up but felt my body couldn't go any more. So we decided that the best idea would be for me to leave my boat there so I would have to come back in the morning no matter what. Then, after a good night's sleep, I could decide whether to pack up and really come home or head out on the river another day. I have never appreciated entering my city and my neighborhood more than I did that night. With each familiar site, I knew I was inches closer to my house. I came home and took a hot shower and many pain pills. I lay in my cozy bed with the air conditioning on full blast and slept like the dead.

Day three upon me, I felt good driving back to the launch. I had slept! In air conditioning no less. And no noisy roosters roused me. And either the pain medicine was working or my body was getting used to paddling more than fifteen miles a day. When I got to the launch site, I was pretty sure that I could make it. Then, when we had our morning safety briefing, I learned about the Class 1 rapids that we would be traversing on that day's stretch, which meant that there would be a lot of current to carry me downstream. I was sold. That day, I felt the best I had since I started. After about ten minutes of paddling, I was getting into my groove; my muscles loosened up, and the current quickened. The rapids seemed to be whirlpools, pulling my boat and swirling me forward through the L-shaped curve. The guides on the trip positioned themselves to help anyone who needed it and to help prevent capsizing. The water gleefully danced around my boat, the three guides screaming, "Paddle, paddle, paddle!" I ended up in a pool of still water, an eddy, coming to rest with my fellow paddlers until everyone made it through the rapids. I rested for fifteen minutes, eating my shark-shaped gummy snacks meant to give me energy, before continuing onward. I was content.

But somewhere along the way, around the city of Reading, several of us in the group noticed that the water turned a deeper shade of brown, and the unmistakable smell of sewage filled our nostrils with every deep breath we took. Some people didn't seem bothered by the smell or the change in the water's turbidity, because they continued to shoot one another with their bilge pumps, which were intended to remove water from their boats but were being used more like Super Soaker water guns. I quickened my paddling to avoid any germ-ridden splashes aimed in my direction and to try to get away from the smell.

I overheard folks chatting throughout the day that the three days we'd done so far were kind of easy compared to what was ahead of us. As we got closer to the city, because of the increase in dams and portages, there would be much flat, placid water. *Egad*, I thought. I really wanted to paddle into Philadelphia so I could have my grand realization of how much I loved my city as soon as I saw it from a different perspective. I decided I needed to rest to regain my strength for the final leg of the trip. Three days and fifty miles down, only eighty to go. I would miss thirty-one and a half miles by taking days four and five off, but I was okay with that. I would rejoin the group on day six. I wanted to kayak into Philadelphia. At the end of the day, I packed up my boat and told my fellow kayakers I'd rejoin them in two days downstream.

Days four and five I left my bed only to use the bathroom and walk my dog. Otherwise, I remained prone, a bottle of pain pills by my side.

Day six. I was rested, rejuvenated and ready for flat water. The sky was the color of the Caribbean Sea with a few cotton ball puffs of clouds. The sun beat down. The day consisted almost entirely of slogging through flat water and portaging around dams. The shores showed battle scars of erosion, covered with invasive Japanese knotweed. At one point, I realized that I was the last boat, right in front of the sweep boat, which is there to guide any paddlers who might be in harm's way. One of the guides paddled over to me to check in. He then tried to convince me that my slowness wasn't really my fault. It was my short, fat boat. My kayak was about ten feet long and about as wide as a canoe. I bought it because it would be stable and prevent me from capsizing in turbulent water. And it was great for going through the rapids. It was, however, very difficult to move in flat water. He recommended renting a longer, thinner boat for the last day of the trip as we paddled into Philadelphia and the lake-like water formed by the Fairmount Dam. And so I did.

Philadelphia was actually the first city to consider water delivery a responsibility of the government. The first water pipes made of hollowed-out logs delivered water from the Schuylkill River to residents of what is today known as Center City. Philadelphia's Water Works was even used as a model by about thirty other cities. The city wisely purchased land along the Schuylkill in an effort to protect the integrity of its drinking water. Today, that area is one of the largest urban parks in the country, known collectively

Kayakers paddle by the Girard Street Bridge in Philadelphia. *Photo by Dave Tavani.*

Kayakers pass by West Philadelphia with the Philadelphia Zoo balloon in the background. *Photo by Dave Tavani.*

as Fairmount Park. The Schuylkill River got its name from Dutch settlers and translates to "hidden river," due to the fact that it was allegedly hidden by deep vegetation at its confluence with the Delaware River. During the 1800s, a trip to the City of Brotherly Love was not complete without a visit to the architectural wonders of the waterworks and the Fairmount Dam. In 1821, the year the dam was built, it was the longest dam in America. To me at this point, it was the enemy.

Day seven was like the last week of school to a high school senior. After a morning portage, all the boats lined up along a concrete barrier on the shoreline waiting for the entire group to catch up. I looked up to see the word "CODA" scrawled in giant graffiti letters on a concrete barrier to the river. How fitting, I thought. The song had played on for the past six days and today was my final passage, bringing this arrangement to a gratifying close. CODA. When I saw the looming radio, television and cellphone towers near the city limits, I was overjoyed. This was my city! Billboards along the interstate overlooking the river had never looked so beautiful. And then I saw it: the Lincoln Drive/Germantown exit on an I-76 bridge marking the exit I take to get to my home.

When the city skyline first came into perspective, I paused momentarily to appreciate it, not because of the beautiful horizon the buildings provided, but because I knew I was almost finished. One landmark after another made me giddy: the East Falls Bridge, Laurel Hill Cemetery, the Girard Avenue Bridge and, finally, Boathouse Row. With each stroke I saw the skyline getting closer. At the end of our destination, we lined our boats across the span of the Schuylkill to take a picture with the city in the background. Seeing the city from the water was a small beacon of hope rising out of the waters. Unfortunately, I was just too tired to enjoy it. When I floated to the dock marking the end of the trip, Dave was there to take pictures and help me with my boat. I had made it, even if I had only paddled 79 of the 110 miles.

I loved Philadelphia so much at that point, mainly because it contained my bed. But there was more to my love than that. I had spent five days in serious pain with a soggy crotch and blisters blossoming on both of my hands and feet just to try to see the city from a different perspective. But all I felt when I came off the water that day was the feeling that I was finally home. Home. In my place. My beautiful city. At that moment, there was nowhere else I wanted to be.

Lots 151-152, Section 14, South Laurel Hill

Philadelphia

By Diana Morris Bauer

My father figured he had not been to Laurel Hill Cemetery in probably fifty years. For Father's Day, I had driven him to the resting place of his grandfather and name source, Elliston, an eighth-generation Philadelphian whose ninety-five years had broadly straddled the nineteenth and twentieth centuries and who lived out his final years in the house of my father's youth. As Philadelphia's first rural cemetery, Laurel Hill's thirty acres hang dramatically above a steep rock face that tumbles down to the swift Schuylkill River, appropriately picturesque for the well-heeled nineteenth-century families who buried their dead some three miles outside the city boundaries at the time, rescuing their loved ones from the overcrowded, anonymous urban graveyards that became increasingly disturbed as industry and housing demands rose. A predecessor to the natural wilderness of Fairmount Park, Laurel Hill offered Victorian-era Philadelphians a Saturday afternoon stroll through its carefully cultivated arboretum appointed with triumphant stone angels signaling heavenward, meticulously tended family plots enclosed by low iron fencing and the affluent miniature city of mausoleums known as "Millionaire's Row."

Visitors could escape the city's confines without confronting the roughness of untamed nature, bringing along a picnic lunch to share with the cemetery's peaceful denizens, strolling easily with children in tow along the park's pleasingly serpentine pathways. At this time, so great was the number of weekend visitors that the cemetery company eventually had to restrict guests to lot holders only. Today, the city's expanse has completely girdled the cemetery, and Laurel Hill feels strangely isolated, an everlasting refuge that seemingly gravitates on its own ethereal plane somewhere above the unbounded tracts of narrow row homes and gray, rumbling traffic that speeds over Ridge Avenue's hard asphalt.

My father and I were the only visitors to Laurel Hill that sweltering June day. Our car passed through the portico of the cemetery's towering Doric gatehouse and slowly navigated this landscape of the dead hovering strangely above our temporal one—a rolling grassy expanse perforated by sharp obelisks jabbing at clouds and family clusters of low, gray headstones arranged like gapped teeth. We sought the marker for my great-grandfather, Elliston Morris, MD. As long as he had lived in the city, he had tended the family plot every Easter, laying wreaths or planting tulips. He visited his two spouses—the youthful bride, Elise, who died young, leaving him to raise two boys, and then his new wife and helpmate, Elise's cousin Josephine—who now lie on either side of him. All three are identical stone markers just at the edge of the narrow lane where I parked the car and left the comfort of air conditioning for the oppressive heat and humidity. My father and I were, however, strangely without ritual, our visit motivated more by family history than duty to the dead. My father took the few steps from our car, rubbing the nearly all-gray hair on the back of his head, thinner every year. He is the last of this tapering family line, Elliston MD's final namesake. My father still sports a bold "III" following his signature, a designation as imposing as the cemetery's towering gatehouse columns yet completely meaningless since he is the last to perpetuate the Christian name. I should have been his son.

We chatted in scant words about his grandfather, whose journals I had recently been reading, and then attended to the other monuments in the family plot, previously beyond our concentration. I reached into the car, pulling out the maroon-bound copy of our family genealogy we brought along. We went to work on the grave-marker inscriptions on the monuments surrounding my great-grandfather, haphazardly at first until we found ourselves turning back to the same page: James, Israel and Galloway, three of Caspar Morris's sons, great-grandfather Elliston's father and uncles. This thread unspooled to reveal the conjoined burial plots of three brothers: James, Israel and Galloway, the first to be interred in Laurel Hill. As we puzzled together this family arrangement, the faces belonging to these graves gradually lifted themselves from the marble and became photographic before our eyes. These are the same brothers who had posed together for two portraits set at least a half century apart, first as children and then as gray old men; both portraits still hang in the foyer of my parents' suburban Philadelphia tract house.

In the youthful photograph, the eldest boy, James, sits on the left, perhaps fourteen or fifteen years old—smart, ready to leave behind the childhood of his two younger brothers and begin his formal education. His left arm wraps around the shoulder of Israel, who, although two years younger, looks

The Morris brothers as boys. *From left to right*: James, Israel and Galloway.

wiser. Israel's eyes, soft and nimble, anchor the picture's tight composition, trained directly on the camera's lens. His right arm rests lazily on his thigh, while his left hand cups the youngster, Galloway's, shoulder. Galloway, with ruinous movement about to release from his lips, stills himself for the long photographic exposure by resting his chin on his palm, his bent elbow firmly planted on the watchful Israel's knee. All three wear white pants and snowy starched collars, the clothing of city youths unaccustomed to sullied labor. James and Israel's forms fill their vests neatly buttoned at the rib cage, their collars encircled by spotless white cravats draped over pristine white shirts. The boys' dark jackets contrast the ivory shimmer on their cheeks, a ghostly illumination on their visages caught by the camera's exposure. Their clothes are the fine, unadorned raiment of the affluent. Only little Galloway, perhaps eight or nine years old, has forearms and chest studded with brass buttons, prescient precursors to fasteners that in another twenty years would ornament his Civil War Union blues. Perhaps off camera stood the parents who arranged this tableau of brotherhood, the anxiety of their children's survival against accident and disease replaced by expectations of greatness. The boys' eager gazes reflect this readiness.

Much later, maybe even a half century later, the three sit once again, this time old men humorously reassembling themselves in the same pose as before. Dark and weighty suits define their forms, and their black ties lie partially obscured under long, grizzled beards. This reenactment serves as a tribute to a long life well lived, the parents who posed them as youths now long dead. Once again on the left, James, a doctor like his father before him, perhaps seventy-five years old now, has somewhat relaxed his mien and sits as a pillar of satisfied service, two fingers of his right hand gently reaching the younger old man's knee, his brother Israel, who remains the intent anchor of this second photograph. Israel, the successful broker, now supports a stature taller than his older brother James. In this later photo, Israel's left arm now rests on rather than restrains a bemused Galloway's shoulder. Galloway, the coal dealer, nearing seventy himself, still concentrates on suppressing an incipient smile, its movement subtly visible in his rising cheeks and narrowly arching eyes. All three now wear practical dark vests with the gold links of watch fobs reaching for vest pockets nestled along their ribs. The triangle shapes of their stiff white shirts beneath the dark suits reach down for their hearts. The expectancy, hunger and mystery once in the eyes of the boys positioned in the first photo have been replaced by satisfaction and comfort. Today, at Laurel Hill, they all lie contentedly, brother by brother, in the quietude of eternal earth perched above the swiftly rushing Schuylkill River.

The same brothers as old men.

Galloway, the youngest, preceded to the grave those born before him, his burial marked by a rough Adirondack granite monolith formed through millennia in the earth, as was the coal he supplied from his Walnut Street office. Israel's wise, protective eyes lie reposed in an elegant, polished-marble cradle topped with the form of a supine cross, following in death less than a year after the younger Galloway he once watched over. James, the eldest, was the last to rejoin this kinship. He now lies under an imposing, broad marble fundament, one vertical surface of which is marked with the bold, even letters of the family name. Each man is now joined by his beloved wife, as well as by the remains of children of a year or a lifetime.

Lots 151–152, Section 14, South Laurel Hill Cemetery, Philadelphia, Pennsylvania.

These three left their names in the marble markers of Laurel Hill, as well as in institutions of the city—University of Pennsylvania, the Academy of Natural Sciences, the College of Physicians—adding to their forbears' distinctions as governor, revolutionary captain and civic and financial leaders. For my father, however, now himself an aging man gazing at the pillars of the dead in front of him, these images carry not only pride but also failed expectations and rebuke. Just as nineteenth-century wealthy Philadelphians searched for a bucolic home for their dead in Laurel Hill, my father's parents eventually sought a home for the living beyond the crowded city limits to raise their children. They found it in the suburban Main Line, an easy rail trip away from urban congestion into hilly estates and spacious custom homes along tree-lined avenues. My grandparents honored the family bulwarks among the dead and reared their children in a tradition of expectation laid out before them in generations of distinction. In the dark library of my father's boyhood home, the two framed photographs of these brothers joined nine other generations of ancestors' portraits immortalized in shimmering oil as well as in photographic sepia tones. As a boy, when my father disappointed his parents, he was made to sit silently and alone beneath these stately gazes to contemplate his shame, a china mantel clock ticking away the measured minutes of his solitary sentence. The ancestors' lofty images stretched toward the ceiling, and my father cowered under their condemning eyes, never growing to add his name to a city institution or even to a university roster. Unable to lay to rest these faces of condemnation, he failed to achieve status, lost hold of the family Adirondack camp where he spent idyllic boyhood summers and even failed to pass on his name a fourth time to a son of his own.

In the oppressive heat, I follow next to my father, whose weakening steps amble away from the family plot over Laurel Hill's grassy lawn and down toward the cliff face above the river for a long view through the humid haze toward the city. As I look to my father's lined face, I see in his eyes a defeated and haunted nostalgia for his forebears, who founded the city towering to the south, an immovable representation as permanent as the grave markers surrounding us of what greatness should have been.

The Philadelphias

Philadelphia

By Heather E. Goodman

As a child, I loved two Philadelphias.

The Philadelphia I saw once a year, every Friday after Thanksgiving, was glitzy, polished. Mom dressed my younger brother Travis in little boy suits or sweaters, me in frills, tights and black patent leather. A necklace but no pierced earrings because her father, my Pop Pop, said that was cannibalism. To this day, Mom's ears aren't pierced, though now mine are. If he were still alive, would I be willing to disappointment him? I doubt it. His praise was sustenance. We got three "Hip-hip-hoorays!" for finishing all the food on our plates, broad smiles for catching flounder or blue fish. He was tall and smelled good, took me crabbing and wrote me notes, and I didn't want any of it to stop ever.

On those Black Fridays, Mom, Dad, Trav and I hustled past City Hall, too close to see William Penn, who really did look like he was peeing—a hilarious joke, we thought. Rushing under City Hall arches hung with wreaths lit in golden light, my adrenalin, already ramped up, skipped to racing. We were about to see the Eagle. Our grandparents, the monorail, Santa, the light show! We ricocheted to the entrance of John Wanamaker's.

Entering Wanamaker's felt like glimpsing adulthood. Huge limestone columns. Gold, glass doors. The smell of pricey fabrics—leather gloves, cashmere scarves, hosiery, coupled with perfume and makeup, polished glass and marble floors. The stone was bright and clean, and people smiled at us. Adulthood looked and smelled fancy. This one day a year, my mom's family, the Eisters, traded in hand-me-down clothes and homemade rugs for city sparkle.

My other Philadelphia was the Goodman family elevator business Dad's grandfather started on the corner of Callowhill and Percy Street in 1909. Security Elevator Company shared the building with my grandfather's other business in stage equipment. These two companies were well matched in the days when asbestos curtains had come into fashion as a way to curtail a plague of theater fires, because, like elevators, the heavy curtains needed pulley systems. The first-floor shop where elevator parts were repaired had racks of angle iron and steel bar stock, lathes, an electric welder, a cut-off band saw and drill presses. Several of the machines were driven by overhead

Security Elevator Company, 1942.

Security Elevator Company, Callowhill and Percy Streets.

belts. The whole first floor smelled like welding, hot steel and scorched oil and eye-burning paint and mineral spirits.

The second-floor office space smelled similar to the first floor, with the scents of mimeograph ink and triplicate forms mixed in. Desks with stacks of folders were jammed into the hot and cloying space. Clacking adding machines competed with ringing phones and people yelling to one another. Three big drafting tables with stools stood in the back corner with men hunched over them. For Travis and me, the highlight was the red machine that gave bottled Cokes for a dime.

Going to work was fun—most of Dad's side of the family was there. My grandfather and grandmother, great aunt, uncle and a bunch of people I thought I was related to because they were always with the rest of my family. For a long time, I thought my extended family lived at the office. When the Goodmans gathered to eat venison one of the men had hunted or for fried sunnies, bass or eel we'd caught on the Lehigh earlier that day, I watched the crowd, wondering why they weren't wearing work clothes.

To my child mind, the office space where Dad spent most of his time was a chaotic, blue-collar version of *WKRP in Cincinnati* meets *Sanford and Son* but with a lot more swearing and jarring. The personalities were just as large as anything on TV: Slater, six-foot-six and fluctuating between 350 and 400 pounds, came on as a truck driver and worked up to be part of the union in the field. Radar, given the nickname by the guys in the field because he had a lazy eye, was fired five times by Security Elevator but continued to come back as a truck driver. Radar's brother, Sonar, was more of a screw-up and didn't last long. Marilyn and Carol, with their nasal Philly accents and huge bodies draped in sweaters, laughed and cackled. My sassy grandmother, red hair blazing, her smoker's laugh the only thing that might keep her pointed words from stinging, worked beside her sister, my refined great aunt whose careful annunciation and silk shirts never fit that office. Uncle Dale's jokes were the first dirty jokes I ever learned. It looked like a party every time we were there: the yelling and swearing and laughing bouncing off the old brick walls.

Back then, Dad seemed to be laughing with them.

Inside Wanamaker's, I looked at Trav, his red hair and Milky Way of freckles waiting for my signal. We speed-walked, flinging our arms, Mom and Dad behind us calling, "No running!" to the Eagle. He towered. Bronzed and regal, cold and ancient. Every year, we begged to climb him, and every year we were told no. He was so tall we had to stand back at the glass counters to see his beak. I begged to be picked up to pet him.

The Eagle faced the dark, soaring wall where the organ stood, and soon the light show began. As a kid, I never realized multiple shows happened on that, or any other, night. It was so special, I thought it only happened once, and we got to be there. If I stood by the Eagle and dropped my head back, I could see all the way up the columned atrium to the eighth floor, where we would visit Santa. Customers jostled around us purchasing clothing and jewelry, toys and picture frames, but none of the Eisters ever shopped.

Though Mom's entire family would meet us at the Eagle, only Nan, Pop and Grandnanny were there when we arrived, the rest even later than we were every year. Trav and I relished in extra hugs, and we conducted long soliloquies about the trains we hoped Santa would set up again in the basement of Nan and Pop's house. Then Aunt Barbara, Uncle Rob, cousins Laura and Steve arrived. I forgot the Eagle and studied cool cousin Laura, seven years older than me and a teenager. I wished

I had her feathered hair and makeup, so I imitated her laugh, her hand movements, trying on teenhood. A few minutes later, Aunt Kathy, Uncle John, Julie and Tracy arrived. Another round of hugging, and the noise escalated. Again, I wanted to be a kid as Julie and Tracy begged to climb the Eagle, too.

We piled into the elevators, fought over who would push the "eight" and made faces at one another in the polished surfaces. The doors opened, and we rounded the corner to Legoland, but the huge planes, cars and robots all built of Legos couldn't stall us. By the time we broke into the toy department, we searched the ceiling for the red and silver monorail, and no amount of calling from our parents could stop us from sprinting. We darted past Barbies, crossbows and catapults and matchboxes to get to the ramp that led all the way up to the ceiling. Even cool cousin Laura dashed up the wooden ramp covered in black rubberized mats, footsteps thundering. We lined up with the appropriate amount of pushing and shoving, except Laura, who protected cousin Tracy, the youngest of us. We squeezed into our seats, sticky in places, the whole train smelling of hot engine and metal. We wrung our fingers through the graphed heavy-gauge wire at the windows. From our vantage point, the ceiling of the toy department, we could see all the displays and shoppers, and we shouted to our family and to one another about what toys we would look at after the ride.

Wanamaker's monorail, the Rocket Express.

Never once did we look at any of them. We just got off, ran down the ramp, begged our parents to go again and ran back up. The monorail was no thrill ride. It hitched and choked its way over the ceiling, each turn seeming to be its last. But the perspective was so unique—a toy department from the ceiling—that we couldn't stop.

Until it was time to see Santa.

Even now, every Christmas, Mom hangs in the living room the photographs taken from these years. In the early pictures, Travis cries. Middle years, we're both pretty cute with various missing teeth. By the end, I'm looking just as gawky and knobby kneed as I felt, with wicked big hair.

Beyond the toy department, the line to Santa snaked through his workshop, where slow-moving, motorized elves worked behind glass, building, polishing, laughing. Santa's lap was hot. And itchy. And he was sweaty, and sometimes his eyebrows were black. I forgot what I'd wanted to ask for.

The inevitable letdown of seeing Santa meant it was finally time to race back downstairs to the light show. Because we'd ridden the monorail too many times, we couldn't get as close to the Eagle as we wanted, and we had to stand near the glass cases with folded shirts. Back then, we were allowed to sit on the glass cases, a whole line of cousins with aching necks and giddy smiles.

Eisters watching Wanamaker's light show, 1978.

The screen went black, and the announcer, whom I presumed was Santa, told us to get ready. The music started. Colored streams of water danced across the bottom. The tree lit up. The Nutcracker fell in love, clocks chimed, Rudolph led the sleigh! Then the blaring train whistle that sounded dangerous and scary. Frosty arrived and too quickly melted. The children's chorus sang "goodbye" as Frosty, one arm waving, faded, and I tried not to cry. Then the music crescendoed, and everything was lit—it was true—Christmas was coming!

Afterward, we went out to dinner at Charlie's on City Line Avenue, where we all sat at one long table, kids at one end, adults at the other. And always, always, we'd had so much fun and worn ourselves out so entirely that I pushed two chairs together or crawled under the table and went to sleep.

Dad carried me out to the car, and though I wanted to stay awake to see all the Christmas lights, the bright city fading behind us, and experience the romantic feel of the cold coming through the window, the car heat of the Pontiac ticking, all four of us bundled in the car, safe and protected, the rumble of tires on road, thinking again and again, *Christmas is coming*—all of it lulled me to sleep.

———

In 1982, Security Elevator Company moved to Fairmount Avenue, a few blocks from the then abandoned and vandalized Eastern State Penitentiary and across the street from vacant row homes. The industry had changed from fixing parts to replacing them, so Security was no longer reliant on a shop to fabricate goods. The first floor housed the heavy-duty electric welder, cut-off band saw, a couple drill presses and the welding table, but mostly it was used as temporary storage for parts and as secure parking for three delivery trucks. Most of the machinery at the Fairmount office was left in place or sold for junk.

Upstairs, the new office was four times the size of the old building's office. Pumpkin orange cubicles stood on grayish brown industrial carpeting, and two whole rows of flip-front file cabinets loomed over me. This is where I spent much of my time, alphabetically filing work orders. There was also a fantastic new copier. My grandfather taught Travis and me how to squeeze our eyes shut and copy our faces. Every time Travis and I went to work, we laid our faces down on the glass and saw the hot yellow light come through our tightly shut eyelids. We signed the copies of our faces and left them as notes for my grandparents. The new office was so fancy it had a sink and a refrigerator.

Beyond the offices was a huge green mottled linoleum floored space, dark and dank and smelling like basement, empty except in the back, where rows of old file cabinets slouched. This is where I spent the rest of my time. My grandfather offered to bring a radio back to me, as he thought I might be bored, but with all that space, my fantasies of future high school dances and curtained stages kept me company as I filed work orders according to completion date.

There was a third floor, where we almost never went. I wanted to live there. The floor was only as large as the last filing room, but it was entirely empty. The huge wood-plank floors must have been the originals, and wide factory windows looked out onto the parking lot. From there, I stared across the street and imagined restoring one of the dilapidated row homes, painting its shutters, window casings and decorative cornices. The room was another great place for daydreaming and dancing around. Here I was free of my gawky preteen body. My hair flew behind me as I sprinted from one end to the other. My knees were always perfectly straight in my cartwheels and back-walkovers. My split and stag leaps were ten feet off the ground. Until someone found me, and then I went back to filing.

Dad worked crazy hours. To avoid traffic, he left the house by 6:00 a.m. He arrived home between six and seven o'clock at night. He worked all day Saturday and some Sundays. I watched as I grew older, and the office became less cool. The city kept Dad away, turning him quiet and easily frustrated and making Mom have to be responsible for everything at home. On the days I worked with Dad, I relished the commute because we talked about the passing scenery, what fish we would catch come spring, what sketch he was thinking about drawing when he had a free hour. Sometimes I could convince Dad to leave the office during lunches. Pete's Famous Pizza, just a few blocks down, was our favorite. We usually ate there, happy to have the pizza loaded because Dad had taught me to love anchovies. Every once in a while we got the pizza to go and ate at Fairmount Park near Lipchitz's *The Spirit of Enterprise*, a scary, warped statue that stood out more than any of the others on our commute along Kelly Drive.

⸺⸱⸺

The last trip to Wanamaker's was five months after Pop Pop died from a heart attack, the family raw and grieving. My cousin Jeff, who was born just before Pop died, would take his first monorail ride in his sister's arms. I was twelve. Wanamaker's was losing ground to other department stores, and though it still retained the family name, the family had sold the company. We didn't know it then, but that was to be the monorail's last year.

I ran up the black rubber ramp. I squeezed myself into the monorail. I was too tall, and the employee shouldn't have let me on, but maybe the teenager felt sorry for me, wanted me to have one more chance at childhood. I no longer was so intoxicated by the smell of adulthood, catching glimpses of it and noting that too often, it neither smelled nor looked good.

That last ride on the monorail was hot and claustrophobic and sad. Pop was gone. Mom was weepy. The metal at the windows wasn't enough to keep me out or in.

———◦———

Security Elevator was bought out by Dover in 1991 as we still mourned the too recent death of Dad's dad. The business moved again. By this time, Dad, Uncle Dale and their colleague Paul ran Security. For this move, they would just need office space. Production would occur in one of Dover's factories. As Wanamaker's had been absorbed, so had Security Elevator.

A ton of old documents needed sorting. Dad found old photos of my great-grandfather and the men who worked with him at Security Elevator.

One photo shows my great-grandfather and four other employees standing on a wooden sidewalk by an entrance to Security Elevator. My great-grandfather poses with his motorcycle. The men don't smile. One stands with his arms crossed. There are metal grates on the bottom half of the windows. This, I remember, was true for the Fairmount office as well.

In a shot from 1942, the men wear suits and hats, even the shop guys. They pose with a roll of steel cable and sheaves. A 1939 Plymouth with the company's logo "Security Service Satisfies" is parked nearby. In the foreground are cobble streets and trolley tracks. On the back is a letter on Security stationery listing the people in the photograph and others who worked there at the time. Among the twenty-six names are several other Goodmans and Braselmans, my great-grandmother's family. The last words on the list: "and Jr. part time." That was my grandfather. My dad is a third. My brother has his own name; early on, my parents were trying to give us more than any other generation had had.

For better and worse, this Philadelphia is long gone.

With the buyout came my freedom. Unless I chose to, I would never have to face a lifetime of work orders, lawsuits and workman's comp—some claims agonized over for the pain friends suffered, a few entirely vexing as evidence revealed the company was being swindled. But where I had gained my freedom, my father had lost his. His days started even earlier; nights ran even longer. His weekends were given to the office or the home computer. Mom, too, losing what little freedom she'd begun to claim as she again became, nearly, a single mom.

As the oldest cousin on my dad's side, many times I had imagined myself sitting at my father's desk, the mountains of files and the nonstop phone my own. I thought I could do it. I would do it. I was a good girl, and I had been given so much by the hands of Security: a house in the woods, a great school district, gymnastic lessons, college. I wasn't sure Travis would join me; he seemed too aware of the wider world and too hungry to miss out on it. But I thought my cousin Justin might take on Uncle Dale's role. My younger cousins, Josh and Georgia, were hardly old enough to remember elevators as a family business.

But I didn't want to learn tax law and accounting software. I didn't want to work weekends for a job I hadn't chosen. I didn't want to wear pant suits and go to conventions and suffer through court trials. I sure as hell didn't want to leverage my house as collateral for the business's insurance, risk losing everything if someone decided to sue, as my parents and aunt and uncle had been forced to do.

Still, even then, before Walmarts and CVS and other chain retailers were forcing mom and pops out of business, before it was so apparent that every town in America was going to look the same if we didn't change our habits, I felt the loss of all that my great-grandparents, grandparents and parents had sacrificed. It felt too easy to be letting it all go. It felt too lucky and too unfair.

Now I could go to college and major in anything I wanted. I could become a journalist, a teacher, study literature, learn to write.

No longer did Dad have to haul all the way into the city. The new office was on the Schuylkill Expressway, just beyond King of Prussia. The building could be seen from 76, and by then I was driving to my own jobs, helping less at Security Elevator as I prepared, with relief, for a career that wouldn't mean running the family business. Still, I waited for the lettered sign on the building. With pride I read Security Elevator Company. But it was a different beast. It was a corporation, no longer a family business, and those years seemed to be the most brutal of all on my dad. He worked every hour he was awake, and he slept little. He didn't sing or fish or sketch. He didn't look at the scenery as he drove to work. The night it was just the two of us at the new office and the payroll software blew up again, he threw a chair at the computer. My father, who'd taught me to nurse a baby raccoon, release fish back to their lakes, look for delicate trout lilies by stream banks. The business was killing him. He retired.

On YouTube, I found a video of the light show I remember from the '80s. Tears came to my eyes watching it. There's a newer version now, with more lights and a different narrator, and I'm glad that new waves of children have it as a memory of their own, but it's not my light show, nor my brother's or cousins'.

Also on YouTube, a video of a father who must be about my age, describing to his children the monorail that lies like a slain dragon in the Please Touch Museum. The kids are distracted and uninterested as he tells them about seeing Santa and riding around the ceiling of the toy department, and why shouldn't they be? The monorail is stationary and on the ground in front of them. The graphed metal at the windows is gone. As the video ends, one of the kids says, "I can see McDonalds, Dad."

The old Wanamaker's building is one hundred years old. The world's largest pipe organ is still there. The light show still plays. Santa still visits. The Eagle still stands. Michael J. Lisicky published *Wanamaker's: Meet Me at the Eagle*. Wanamaker's is more history than present.

Only in hindsight did I realize that the only money the Eisters ever spent on those Black Fridays was for the Santa photograph and dinner. It all seemed so rich. And it was—just not in the way of marble and glass and polish. And it was decadent because we never all went out to dinner—neither did the Goodmans—but that one night a year; the rest of the year we crammed around my grandparents' table in their small house in Havertown, eating blue fish we'd caught or sitting on the floor with my grandmother's ham and egg salad sandwiches cut in quarters.

My parents are artists. High school sweethearts, they grew up in small post–World War II houses, where frugality meant working hard and play meant providing that night's dinner. Throughout my life, Dad has sketched and carved and made beautiful furniture in his spare time, which was basically on vacations. Mom takes photographs that rival magazine glossies, but these photos are almost always taken at weddings or birthdays or to commemorate someone else's event. While we were growing up, there was no time for her own photography subjects—she was running the family, the house, working as a librarian, volunteering at our schools. Before Mom and Dad retired, these pursuits were given the few free hours of a vacation, the few free minutes of a weekend.

What they have given me, what the glitz and grease of my Philadelphias have given me, is the confidence and ability to choose my own path. They gave me an education, a profession of my choosing and, out of that, the realization that going into business for myself would give me the gift of time to practice my art every day, not just on vacation. One Philadelphia has helped me see I don't want fine leathers and silk, but I desperately want time—time my grandfathers never had, time my parents are only starting to have now that they're retired. The other Philadelphia gave me the means to pursue this goal.

When non-natives come to visit, I point out with pride Boat House Row, the Art Museum, Independence Hall. I don't explain Callowhill, Wanamaker's, Fairmount. It's too complicated, too overwhelming, too bittersweet.

Every time I get into an elevator, I check to see who made it. A few Dovers still remain, but they, too, were bought out, so mostly the elevators are made by an old competitor or new international companies. The last Dover I was in was at the parking garage of the DoubleTree on Broad Street. The plasticized one- by sixteen-inch sign had been mangled and jutted from the wall of the elevator; the opposite wall revealed a perfect new sign of the company that bought out Dover. One side of the mangled sign read Dover; on the other side it read Security Elevator Company. I was alone. I grabbed the sign, twisted and tugged, and it popped off. I gripped it in my fist. The doors opened, and I walked out.

The SEPTA Stranger

Philadelphia

By Deborah Good

I have lived twenty-four of my thirty years in large, East Coast cities—in D.C. for sixteen and now in Philadelphia for eight—and have somehow managed to fall short of *fashionable* and *polished*. I am more likely the woman sprinting down the sidewalk for a train, a heavy shoulder bag flopping against my back and a plastic grocery bag ripping at its handles because of the soccer cleats and shin guards inside. Sometimes I am the one stepping into the library wiping moisture from my forehead where a subtle bike-helmet imprint lingers, my hair slightly matted from the commute. I have often spent my summers looking sweaty and a little muddled, not because I am an utter disaster when it comes to yuppiehood—though that is probably true—but because of how I live much of my life: waiting on public transportation, navigating the city on my bicycle and, for blocks and sometimes miles at a time, getting by on foot.

Philadelphia is a "city of neighborhoods," a patchwork of communities with distinctive personalities, histories of strength and tribulation and a hodgepodge of loyal, longtime residents. The neighborhoods are connected by a web of buses, trolleys, subways and trains—collectively called the Southeastern Pennsylvania Transportation Authority, but better known among locals as *fucking SEPTA* due to the system's inadequacies and proclivity for lateness.

Eight years in Philadelphia have taught me the art of piecing together a day's worth of getting from here to there, using any combination of SEPTA,

Trolley, West Philadelphia. *Photo by Ryan Good.*

biking, walking, catching rides with friends and—once I'd bought my first car—driving myself. There is a method to the plan-making. I weigh cost, parking options, timing, efficiency and accessibility. Ideally, I take into account gas prices and my carbon footprint. I gauge my own lethargy. I make all sorts of compromises, so I am often late.

On one trek from my neighborhood in West Philadelphia to another in the Kensington area of the city, I locked my bike at a train stop, rode the R3 from Forty-ninth Street to Center City and then transferred to the Blue Line, which is also called the "El." Shortly after I'd found my seat, a man parked himself beside me and launched into conversation.

"I went to the University of Pennsylvania to have caps put on my teeth." I smiled and turned to look at him. "But later that day," he continued, "they fell off, and I swallowed them."

"Oh, really?" I managed to spit out.

"So I went to my doctor, who said they would pass. But they didn't pass and they didn't pass." By this point, my smile took up much of my face. "And so I had an endoscopy done. They eventually had to cut them out of me."

"Wow—"

"And the crazy part about it is that my insurance covered the endoscopy and surgery—but they won't cover my dental, which is why I went to the school in the first place instead of paying for a regular dentist."

I would miss such conversations if I spent summers in my car. Still smiling, I leaned back and slouched, letting my ass slide forward on the cool, hard plastic of my seat. I wondered at the unexpected connection with a SEPTA stranger, especially because the norm on public transit, in my experience, is to stare quietly down or out the window or at an odd spot at the corner of the ceiling. We rarely talk to one another. The man's story, I decided, was brilliant. It had amused me, and just when I was beginning to peg him and his story as little more than strange-but-entertaining jabber, he hit me with his somewhat revolutionary punch line: our systems of healthcare and insurance are sometimes absurdly wasteful and irrational.

My encounter with this stranger on the El reminded me of a story a friend had told me one year earlier: Josh went to work—standing on South Street, inviting passersby to give money to support his organization. A young woman approached him. "How are you today?" he asked her.

"To be honest, I'm kind of sad."

"I'm kind of sad, too," he replied.

"Really? Why are you sad?"

"I'm sad because a friend of mine died last night." He looked at her. "Why are you sad?"

"I'm sad because my boyfriend doesn't love me anymore."

And right there on South Street, two complete strangers gave each other a hug. They stood in the middle of the sidewalk, holding each other for a good minute. Later, she returned with a flower—"I thought you could use this"—and walked on. He never even asked her name. As I sat on the El, I wondered if all the world could be like this: engaged enough to notice and share our grief, selfless enough to comfort one another. I need these stories, lest I forget that good and love still exist in the world.

After tunneling beneath downtown, the El emerges on the city's east side and becomes an elevated train, perched on trusses of steel painted blue. The man next to me without dental insurance pulled a weekly from his bag and scanned the classifieds. A teenager sat coolly across the aisle to my right, his shoulder propped against a window; black wires dangled from his ear buds, and the red, white and blue of a Puerto Rican flag peeked out between the folds of his shirt. I glanced past him, toward the Delaware River. The metallic knocking of wheels against tracks produced a familiar, erratic percussion that paused when the train stopped at Spring Garden and then at Girard Avenue.

I rode for two more stops, bid the man-who-swallowed-his-caps farewell—"Have a good one!"—and stepped onto the platform. Once on the street below, I set off on a nine-block walk between the flat faces of Kensington's brick row homes to an urban farm where my housemates and I were members. I lugged a small cooler, and my usual shoulder bag was slung across my back. As Philadelphia's muggy summers are not for the faint of heart, sweat dripped down my legs as I schlepped through one of the worst heat waves of the season.

Most places in the world are full of complexities that trained social scientists and political analysts continually mine for explanations. The Kensington neighborhoods are no different. Historically an industrial center, Kensington is now peppered with abandoned factories left behind when blue-collar jobs moved overseas. The area is home to poor and working-class whites, blacks and Latinos, mostly Puerto Ricans—and is gradually being transformed by an encroaching, gentrifying force. Illicit business transactions take place not far from trendy coffee shops and yoga studios. Young artists have moved in next to longtime Irish residents. Property values are creeping up.

Like the experts, I too am trying to make sense of it all. I read the paper and listen to my fair share of National Public Radio. I read books by people smarter than me, and at my day job, I study urban public education—that inequitable tangle of hope and struggle—as a social researcher. Mostly, though, I prefer to leave the academics to their good research and their banter, while I leave my house to walk, ride or bus the streets they analyze. When I return from my escapades through the city, I won't be able to recite the percentage increase in homelessness since the year 2000, but I will offer that the woman who asked me for money had short, graying hair and a steady gaze. I can't write a thorough report on the gentrification of the neighborhood where I grew up in Washington, D.C., but I can describe its smell like urine on Irving Street, half a block from the site where six-digit condos have gone up.

I like to tread the landscapes of places I cannot explain and do not understand. Philadelphia's local news programs teach us to fear parts of the city, but when possible, I prefer to breathe in the air of these streets and come home telling my own stories. On this particular walk through Kensington, I tried distracting myself from the pain in my shoulders and the sweat springing from my forehead and armpits. I remembered a recent issue of the *Philadelphia City Paper* for which Duane Swierczynski had his staff explore the city on their own two feet and then write about it. He himself walked a street he had seen rushing by his car window hundreds of times before. "In exchange for an hour of my time—that's how long it took to walk home—everything in an overly familiar stretch of the city looked like I'd just been sprung from jail after ten years," he writes. "Up close, everything was new." This is, of course, the romanticized view.

But he is right. Walking brings me the world more slowly, less insulated and in greater detail. On foot, I have plenty of time to internalize the smells, sounds and conversations I encounter on my way.

I made my way to the urban farm that was my destination and filled my cooler with our household's share of carrots, tomatoes, blackberries, eggs and cream. I then set off on a slightly different route through the neighborhood, back to the El. It was a quiet walk past row houses, small businesses, a few abandoned lots.

I would like to say that my stroll was pleasant and that I was bolstered by my choice to reduce my CO_2 emissions into our ever-warming atmosphere and curtail my gas consumption in its tangle with global politics and war. But it was not pleasant, and I was not bolstered. I was hot, my cooler was heavy and I could not wait to get home. After four and a half blocks, I stopped at a small stand to buy a cup of mango-flavored water ice. Grateful, I let the thin, plastic spoon rest on my tongue for

Downtown skyline, Philadelphia. *Photo courtesy www.conraderb.com.*

a minute before the sweet, orange liquid slid off and down my throat, cooling the sides of my esophagus.

I finally made it back to the El platform, boarded the train when it arrived, transferred at City Hall to the 34 trolley and made my way by foot the last three blocks to the West Philadelphia home I shared with friends. I would have to rescue my bicycle—still locked to a metal railing at the Forty-ninth Street R3 stop—sometime later, the one imperfection in the day's walking/biking/public transit plan. In the meantime, I unloaded the contents of the cooler onto the counter at home and into the refrigerator. I grabbed a chilled beer from the back of the second shelf and rolled the glass bottle up and down the back of my neck. I turned on a fan and stared straight into it, panting like a puppy.

Yankee Land

Philadelphia

By Jillian Ashley Blair Ivey

I'd been clinging to my Texas driver's license for seven years, since I moved to West Philadelphia to attend the University of Pennsylvania. As I walked through the ivy-covered campus, shaded by the trees lining Locust Walk, it was my ID that set me apart from my schoolmates, mostly privileged New Yorkers and New Jerseyans who had traveled all through Europe but never ventured west of Eastern Standard Time. It gave me credibility when I went with friends to a shooting range. On more than one occasion, it motivated a bartender to pour me a double for the price of a single. It was a conversation topic; it was the last vestige of my Texan-ness.

I didn't have a car while I was in college, so it didn't seem to matter what state's flag flew over my photo when I was asked to show identification. When I graduated, I joined a car-sharing service for trips to the supermarket or IKEA, and its member services department didn't care where my license was from, as long as I had one. But acquiring a boyfriend with a car means acquiring frequent car privileges, and when Ross's insurance agent learned just how frequent, he insisted that, per state law, I get a Pennsylvania license.

This information, delivered to me via a forwarded e-mail in the middle of the workday, was received about as well as a doctor's warning that it's time for a tetanus shot. "Do I have to?"

"Just because of the logistics, or because you're opposed to having a Pennsylvania license on principle?" came Ross's reply.

"Both," I wrote back.

I spent the rest of my afternoon in a funk, and when I got home, I tried to explain to Ross what the card I'd been carrying in my wallet meant to me. It affirmed me as an expatriate; but I was still *from* Texas. After all this time in Philadelphia, it felt like the last remnant of my origins, and suddenly some faceless insurance agent was trying to take my Texas away from me.

"But you don't live there anymore." Men can be so sensitive. "It's not like he's asking you to get a new birth certificate."

Ross wasn't going to understand why this was such a big thing for me. He wasn't going to understand that there's a special relationship native Texans have with their state, no matter where they eventually land. I was no exception, even though I had done everything in my power to stay in Philadelphia after college. So here I was, fighting the same fight that so many Texans before me had fought—a fight for my statehood. It was my own mini-Alamo, and I was going to lose.

"Fine," I told Ross. "I'll get a new license."

"Good," Ross said. "The picture on your old one is awful."

———

The envelope was thin, and when I opened it, I sat on the curb down the street from my parents' house and cried. I refolded the letter and shoved the thick, embossed paper into my back pocket, careful that my jacket covered the evidence, then gathered the rest of the mail, wiped my eyes and walked toward home. My dad was backing his pickup truck into its space.

"What's happening, kiddo? Anything good in the mail?"

"Nothing special, Daddy. Catalogues and bills. Need a hand with anything?"

"Nah. Go on inside. Your mom's out, but she'll be back soon."

I raced straight to my room and waited for my mother to get home. When I heard her car in the driveway, I ran downstairs, intercepted her at the garage and handed her the envelope. "You have to tell him. I can't."

I helped Mom unload groceries and slipped back upstairs under the pretense of doing homework but really to let my mother fight my battle for me. I heard the door to my parents' bedroom shut, a sign that their argument might escalate beyond something their daughters should overhear. I tried to study for my physics final but couldn't. It didn't matter. I'd just been accepted at Penn, and early decision at that: admission was binding. My final grades would only matter if I failed.

Dad called my name; I turned my stereo on and pretended I didn't notice. A few minutes later, the door to my bedroom banged open—Dad never knocked. "So, you wanna come down and talk to your parents for a minute?"

I didn't, but I followed him anyway. Mom was sitting on the sofa staring into the fireplace, eyes red—they often were after those closed-door conversations. I sat down beside her; Dad sat across from us on the hearth, elbows on knees, fingertips pressed together and pointed in my direction. "Philadelphia."

"Yes, Daddy."

"Philadelphia?"

"Yes. Dad."

"I hoped you wouldn't get in."

"Can't you just be proud of me? I got into an Ivy League university."

"What's wrong with schools in Texas?"

"Nothing. But anybody else's father would be proud of his daughter getting into Penn."

Dad rattled off the benefits of Texas A&M—his family's school of choice—and the University of Texas, where everyone on Mom's side of the family had gone. "Or hell, if you don't want to stay in Texas, what about Colorado? What about California? Why does it have to be Yankee Land?"

⸎

"Yankee Land" is what my father calls the part of the United States that's both east of the Mississippi River and north of the Mason-Dixon line. For reasons he's never fully explained, he doesn't think too highly of the region or its inhabitants, and he's been trying to convince me to leave it and come back to Texas.

Mom tries to convince me, too, but in more subtle ways. When I was in college, she'd ship boxes of Mexican food ingredients to my apartment—canned green chilies, enchilada sauce, chipotle chilies packed in smoky adobo, fresh tortillas—and pad them with Texas flags, cowboy boot–shaped potholders, "Yellow Rose" bandanas and collections of bumper stickers and notepads urging whoever laid eyes on them not to mess with Texas.

"There was extra room in the box," she'd tell me. A teacher of Texas history to unappreciative fourth graders, she now calls or e-mails on her lunch break with textbook tidbits she thinks I would appreciate better than her students: "Did you know that Texas is the only state allowed to fly its flag at the same height as the American flag? Did you know that today is Sam Houston's birthday?"

The general understanding in my family, myself included, was that I'd move back to Texas after my furlough in Yankee Land. I liked Philly, but it wasn't where I thought I'd settle after graduation. I planned on heading back south, where I found both the climate and the people to be warmer.

But then I got a job. A job that wasn't in Texas. Dad was pleased that my English degree didn't make me completely unemployable but made it clear that when my two-year contract was up, he expected me back in the Lone Star State. When, after nine months, the job didn't work out, he asked if I needed help moving.

I started collecting unemployment instead. I told Mom; she agreed it made sense for me to buy myself some time. I told Dad; he said no daughter of his should be collecting welfare and hung up on me when I tried to explain that it's called unemployment *insurance* for a reason. Mom phoned with a counter-offer: break my lease, fly home, use the family cabin for the summer, rent-free, and do some writing. Tempting, but I wasn't ready to leave Philadelphia yet. I couldn't find good barbecue or Mexican food anywhere, and tequila was ridiculously expensive, but I loved living in Center City. It was the middle of the Philadelphia Film Festival, and baseball season was coming up. I had friends. I had a schedule. I had a life. As long as I could still live that life traipsing through Independence Hall in my Tony Lama cowboy boots and flashing my Texas ID at the beer distributors, that was enough for me.

I thanked my mother for being so thoughtful and told her I was going to pass. I reminded my father that when I graduated, I had committed to staying in Philadelphia through the summer of 2008. My job might have ended, but my plan hadn't.

I continued my Philadelphia life. I started dating Ross. I found another job. After work, I'd sometimes go to Ross's and make dinner—often Mexican food prepared with ingredients shipped from home. He'd come to my place and make fun of the Texas flag trivet hanging over my stove. We'd go out, and bouncers would look at me suspiciously—Texas IDs being notoriously easy to forge—then hold my driver's license under the black light and ask me my zip code. "79912. It's an old picture."

Ross and I got serious, and my scheduled summer 2008 evacuation date seemed increasingly arbitrary. Instead of moving back to Texas, I moved in with him. We found a beautiful two-bedroom apartment in Northern Liberties, walking distance to Liberty Lands Park and the nearly complete Piazza complex. It had wood floors and crown molding and granite countertops and vintage subway tiles on the bathroom walls—and it was just far enough out of Center City that sometimes I needed to borrow Ross's car for simple errands or to get to my graduate classes in New Jersey. His insurance agent said that if I "really was going to stay in Philadelphia"—meaning, if I was going to stay with Ross—I'd better get a Pennsylvania license.

The PennDOT on South Columbus Boulevard was packed. After half an hour in line, the woman at the front desk asked why I was there. "I'm changing my residency."

"Twenty-three dollars. Check or money order? Fill out this paperwork. NEXT!"

I looked at Ross, who'd come along for moral support. "Do you have a checkbook on you?"

"You're the one with the purse."

I dug deep and discovered that I did, in fact, have a checkbook with me. It had one last "Texas" check left, another of my mother's subtle reminders of my heritage. On it, a silhouetted cowboy twirled his lasso under a desert sunset. I showed Ross that I was on the last page. "It's a sign," he said, grinning at me.

I sighed, signed my name and handed the payment to the receptionist, then took a number and sat, waiting the same way I wait for the dentist to call my name: ready to run out the door. Ross held my hand. "You'll still be a Texan, you know."

And then it was my turn. I handed over the required proof of Pennsylvania residency, along with my Texas license, which I'd been told I would need to surrender. I was surprised when the PennDOT agent handed it back to me. "There you go. You can hold on to that. Now, go sit over there and wait for them to call you up for a photo."

I walked back to Ross, proudly waving my old ID. "I get to keep it!"

"See? You can still have Texas in your wallet."

I heard my number and walked up to the photo desk and handed over the slip that certified I met the requirements for a Pennsylvania driver's license.

"I need your old license, too."

"But I thought I could keep it."

The author's temporary Pennsylvania license.

"Don't worry, honey. I just need to see it real quick. Now sit over there and say 'cheese.'" I smiled into the camera, waited for the flash and popped back up.

"I'll call you when your temporary license is ready," the woman said. I started to walk toward Ross. "Wait!" she called after me. "You forgot your old ID." I returned, held out my hand and saw her take out a hole-puncher and hold it over my license. She squeezed down, and suddenly, where the Texas flag once flew over my photograph, there was nothing but a small, round hole.

"What's wrong?" Ross asked me as I shuffled his way and showed him the circular wound PennDOT had inflicted on my sense of self, the insult it had just paid the only state flag that flew as high as America's. I wanted to cry.

"Miss Ivey? Your license is ready. Have a nice day, and congratulations on your move to Pennsylvania."

Welcome to Yankee Land. Population: me.

Delaware and Pine

Philadelphia

By Darcy Cummings

Until I was five years old, my family lived in a nineteenth-century seaman's hotel on the Philadelphia waterfront. During the Depression, my grandmother, a widow, converted the middle two floors of the small hotel—the only property that hadn't been lost when my grandfather went bankrupt—into makeshift apartments with small rooms, one after the other, along the long corridors. There she gathered those in the family who needed a place to live out the hard times. She and my uncles ran the restaurant and bar on the first floor and a gas station on the corner. Living there made me see the world as a series of images rather than events.

My mother was an artist, which contributed to my desire to draw the things I saw in the hotel. When my baby brother Mike was asleep, my mother painted on a large canvas as I sat on the floor trying to draw the pots and blocks she put in front of me. I remember her canvases and the smell of turpentine, paint, coffee and cigarettes, and the waxy feel of the crayon in my hand, its odd smell, the happy feeling of having her to myself during the quiet afternoon. At that age, I owned words but did not know how to get them on paper. It never occurred to me that the words in books were made by someone. Language always seemed weaker than images, and less true.

I can still see vivid images from that period of my life: someone handing me a small, round red pepper and the intense scarlet of my burning hands and lips and eyes after I ate it; a smiling child with no arms, just stumps, in the wading pool of Stanfield playground; and a row of green velvet ring boxes, each

A customer of McClernan's in the 1930s.

containing a beetle, which I had captured in the hallways or on the sidewalk outside our building. Or maybe they were roaches or crickets. My aunt, who had given me the ring boxes, screamed when I showed her my collection. Her reaction to those tiny machine-like things, glossy and skittery, with clever moving parts delighted me. The hotel was surrounded by warehouses, a chicken slaughterhouse, a building with a peculiar dead smell where bales of rags were stored and the thick, gray river. The neighborhood had an odd pitch and scale: a train passed the side of the hotel, and across Delaware Avenue, a wide street no child could ever cross alone—it seemed dangerous even for parents to cross—huge freighters docked at the ramshackle piers that stretched into the oily river. Outside, people seemed small and insignificant. Inside, they seemed too large for the narrow space.

When I tell my children and friends about those years, they seem horrified—what a terrible place, they say. Even in those days, it wasn't a place where families lived. My cousin Billy, who was then eight, on the way home from a store, was attacked by a group of older boys who stole the groceries and change. When a man who found him wandering in a maze of row houses below South Street took him to a nearby police station, the desk sergeant didn't believe Billy when he told them that he lived at Delaware Avenue and Pine Street. No one lives there, the cops told him—only factories and warehouses and docks are around there—no houses or apartments. Luckily, a policeman who knew my grandmother rescued Billy and took him home.

Our home, a fascinating place, shaped me—all of us—for the rest of our lives. The layout made my parents, brother, grandmother, aunts, uncles and cousins feel isolated from the outside world, yet crowded; there was little room or privacy. When I was very young, I sensed all the worries and stories that occupied that building—my grandfather's lost fortune; the three college-educated uncles, my mother's oldest brothers, who'd run away to New Orleans (an engineer, a musician and a businessman, emblems of the family's shattered potential); my father's drinking; the purple scar along my mother's throat. Years later, I learned about the car accident that almost killed her, that killed her friend. The whispered word: "decapitation." The insurance settlement from the accident that left my mother unable to drive for thirty years paid for her wedding dress, a glamorous satin Juliette gown. A picture of my father and her in the gown hung on the wall above the sturdy sofa, also purchased with the accident money. And a set of sterling silver flatware. Twelve place settings. In the depth of the Depression, my mother felt that buying solid silver was a tie to respectability, a link to the good years when my grandfather had properties, a Ford and a restaurant in New Jersey.

On the top floor of the hotel was an unused dance hall my grandmother called a ballroom filled with broken furniture and worn carpets. The first floor—a bar, restaurant and kitchen—was dim, sour and beery in the morning, then filled with men's voices, pianola music and glittering bottles and neon signs at night. From our third-floor window, Delaware Avenue became foggy and gray at night with a red spot from the train lantern

Grandmom McClernan keeping an eye on the neighborhood from the fourth floor of the building in which she and her extended family lived during the Depression.

Harry and Billy McClernan and the author in front of McClernan's in 1939.

glowing beneath a blur of yellow moon. Since the outside world was filled with so much danger, most of our time was spent inside, looking out at the fire escapes, the trucks piled with baled rags and the black men and women who worked in the building down the street plucking feathers from the carcasses of chickens that only minutes before had been noisy and crowded together in barred wooden crates.

One night, I was sitting at the table; my mother was cooking. Behind me, my father's steaming bulk. The gas flame flared and ebbed under a black pot. In front of the stove, the wood floor beneath the worn-through linoleum seemed to be reaching toward the flame. Never touch the stove. My baby brother was painting his face and the highchair with pabulum. On a white plate, a blood orange, which seemed to be on fire. The smell of turpentine mixed with the onions and potatoes. My mother had started a new painting; a smudge of red paint on her face and arm. How to get the ships and river and its sounds all on flat board? A *muh, muh, muh* brother hummed under the clock tick. Then, mother started to fall, slowly, first holding on to the back of a chair, then softly, onto her knees. She lay on the floor, scratching the linoleum's flat roses. My father's chair scraped back. "What, what!" the kettle seemed to scream, "What has he done now?"

Before I began kindergarten, my father got a new job, and we moved to Trenton, to a small working-class neighborhood, with rows of drab bungalows, a park, four cemeteries and a school with a small, beautiful, Romanesque parish church. This was during the war; my father had been transferred to a new milk and ice cream factory, a branch of the dairy he'd worked for in Philadelphia. That was considered an essential industry, so he wasn't taken into the army. When we played outside in summer, sometimes a huge ice cream delivery truck with a sign, ABBOTT'S DAIRIES, would grind to a stop, and the driver would throw us a box of ice cream sandwiches.

No noise, trains, trucks, river, music or smells. We had a yard and trees, a flourishing garden and fields and woods to investigate. But I missed our waterfront home and the pack of bold boy cousins who lived downstairs, the boys I wanted to be like.

My mother, lonely without Grandmom and our other relatives, continued to paint until her third child was born, when my father made her put the oils away and store the paintings and clay figures in the cellar. By that time, I knew all the reasons people became artists, or, at least, why she became an artist: because it made her happy, because she needed to escape from children and diapers and because she was not like the women living around us who spent their days cleaning and cooking.

After she died, I found a journal my mother kept as part of an art course she took when she was in her sixties. One entry reacted to an English psychiatrist's theory of creativity. "I now begin to understand myself and my family, my parents and siblings," and a few pages later, "I have entailed my talent to my children."

My mother and I both missed Delaware Avenue and Pine, for the trips shopping to South Street, crowded with the rows of carts loaded with fruits and vegetables, the short bony men in baggy suits, shills who tried to pull us into the clothing and material stores for sales. "Such a beautiful girly, such blond curls and blue eyes. Lady, we have a dress for her, such a bargain." Sometimes we'd take long walks to Center City, to Franklin Square for a picnic. In Trenton, our mother continued to teach me and my brother to paint and model clay, which distracted me from grieving for our lost odd paradise. Some nights I lay in bed and imagined I was walking with my eyes closed from Delaware Avenue to Second Street at the end of the block: the feel of the cracked, rough sidewalk under my feet. Step by step, I'd retraced the scents—tar, rags, gasoline, beer and roast beef; old, unpainted boards; peppery weeds; and singed feathers. Then, comforted, I'd fall asleep.

———◦———

When I started school, my teachers urged me to write and rewarded me for the words I produced. In the second grade, I wrote a composition called "Colored Feathers," a one-page account of my trips to the chicken pluckers' steamy shed to gather feathers for art projects. The essay won a gold star and a place of honor on the bulletin board. However, the page didn't say everything I'd felt standing in the doorway to the slaughterhouse. I was dizzy with homesickness for Philadelphia, remembering the smell of sweat, singed feathers and blood. Painting made me feel that way.

After a while, my mother's supply of paper and watercolors ran out, and there was no money to buy more. I began drawing on the cardboard that came inside new shirts, which my grandmother saved for me, stolen paper from school and, finally, the blank front and back pages of books, even my mother's books, when she was too distracted to notice. One morning, a car hauling a small silver mobile home shaped like a high turtle pulled up in front of my house. A tall man strode up the walk, followed by a short lady in a fancy dress. I pretended not to notice them. The man watched me drawing for a minute and then growled, "Didn't anyone ever teach you to respect books? Why are you doing that?"

I didn't look up. "Don't have any paper."

"Is your mother home?" The front screen opened, and my mother cried, "Oh, John. Johnny, is that you?" One of my lost uncles, the jazz musician from New Orleans, was found. They hugged and cried and made a lot of noise. He and his wife stayed for three days, sleeping in their metal trailer. At night, he and my mother would stay up late and talk. Every day, my uncle, who had no children, would talk to me about writing and drawing and music. He particularly liked, he said, the drawings of Philadelphia and of princesses in captivity. I fell a little bit in love with him: he was glittery and funny. He played clanky music that sounded just right on our out-of-tune piano. He told me stories of the hotel when he was small, when my grandfather had first owned the building. Although he now lived what sounded like a glamorous life in New Orleans, and he loved that city, he smiled and said, "But Philadelphia…oh, Philadelphia…"

A month later, a big box, addressed to me—only me—came from New Orleans. It was filled with lined pads and watercolor paper, cardboard and poster paint. Erasers, brushes, pencils and a small pencil sharpener. And it was all for me. A note said: "Now you can draw and write all you want, all summer. But not in books. Love from Uncle John and Aunt Mim."

"He was always my favorite older brother," my mother said. We were sitting on the sagging steps to the front porch. We'd opened the box right there. "He left home when I was ten."

"Older than me," I said, snatching paper and pencils from the box.

"He was always kind to me." I looked at her. She seemed very tired, and skinny, though her stomach was fat. Fat again. I grabbed a wooden box filled with jars of poster paints.

"His wife is lucky," she said. "So lucky." Her words were stones, though I don't think they seemed that way then.

"Yeah," I said, staring at the jars of red paint. Four different reds, all with different names. The name of the best red was printed on the lid. I'd never seen that word before. It began with a V, but I didn't, as usual, spell out the word and ask mom how it sounded, what it meant. I held the jar up to the sun. Perfect. The paint was exactly the color of the inside of a blood orange.

Daddy's Glasses

North Philadelphia

By Bernard E.D. Wilson

*T*he first place I called home was a second-floor apartment in the 1900 block of Marvine Street, hard in the shadows of Temple University. The then college had not yet flexed its muscles, nor had it experienced the growth spurt that would eventually consume this small enclave in North Philadelphia.

Marvine, as the entire immediate area was called, was a wonderful place full of interesting characters that reflected vestiges of the old community—mainly eastern Europeans. But its most populous residents were the newly arriving blacks who had recently come from fields to factory jobs in the North and had made this their new home in the final great wave of migration of the 1940s and early 1950s.

These former residents played an integral role in the health and vibrancy of the neighborhood. Jewish merchants selling pigs' feet, hog maws and grits. The redheaded Irishman with the handlebar mustache at the "Yellow Front" hawked the freshest produce imaginable, with trays of mustard and collard greens reposing under the canopy on the sidewalk right next to barrels of black-eyed-peas and okra. Of course, at the time, I had no way of knowing what a tremendous commitment it must have taken for these people and others like them to remain and tailor their trades to the newcomers—personal ethics or taste aside. The only other people we regularly saw who were not of color were the insurance man who sold cheap term-life policies and the Harbison milkman who left the milk on the doorstep long before most folks were awake. All I knew was that these people who did not look like me were as welcome and as essential to the community as was the man who ran the "numbers" and the ones who sold corn liquor.

The interplay between people of other cultures did not in and of itself spell negativity. Had it not been for the efforts of my mother, who undertook a mission to expose me to all that the city had to offer, I would have grown up thinking most of the world outside our little community operated in much the same way. Philadelphia was and remains primarily a city of neighborhoods where folks often have no practical reasons for venturing outside that which they know. As a small, brown child holding the strong hand of a woman who worked hard to make a living for us, I felt much comfort in the strength in those calloused hands and the positivity that radiated from her tired brown eyes. She presented the world that was Philadelphia as a place through which one could successfully maneuver, but caution and a certain sense of "place" were requirements for melanized people.

My uncle's experience was not so positive. As a laborer, not so rosy. In the absence of a father, he became "Daddy" to me, as well as to my two cousins, with whom I grew up as brothers. Often, at the end of a hard day, he came home and told us stories. Some made us laugh and others caused us to lie in our shared beds, trying hard to understand the true meaning in what he had told us. Some of the hard truths were clearly delineated and needed no further explanation. Others, such as the story below, were not so easy to fathom. This story he told in 1957 has never left me.

A construction crew was working on a sewer line in the Burholme section of the city—a part of the Northeast. In that bastion of homogeneity, people of color had found no resting place. Those who lived there did so in celebration of the absence of diversity. This gang of men was laboring especially hard on a hot, humid, typical Philadelphia July afternoon in 1956. Aside from the obvious fact that there is always one man being paid—it would seem—to just stand around and look into the hole while pickaxes, shovels and jackhammers violently rent the roadway, the only other fact of interest was not this disparity of labor but the variations of the colors of the workers' sweat-drenched skin.

The majority of the men, despite labels such as Italian, Greek and Irish, mirrored the neighborhood even though they did not live there: they were white even though they were cast in varying shades of red, gold, bronze and tan, with parts of their exposed anatomies reaching crimson and even maroon from laboring out in the open for most of the summer and many summers long spent.

They made an interesting collection, this cadre of multihued men toiling under the oppressive sun that always shone down but with no respect to person. They were more akin to bees than to mere men. Each one had a particular role to perform. Each one dared not let the other down for fear of verbal reprisal or worse—being "let go" and being replaced by some other equally willing worker.

Among them was a lone black man who cast his shadow to the tarmac with moderately altered hues. The tar-paved roadway reflected the heat and seemed to absorb something of his wearied spirit in the process.

"Johnson, slow down man! What's your rush," the foreman said to the top of Johnson's bent brown head. The man looked back at the speaker with blank, unseeing eyes. The sweat dripped down from the black man's soaked hatband and seemed to run from the corners of his eyes.

"Nothin'," he mumbled.

"What the hell's eatin' him," the foreman asked no one in particular. Several of the gang looked up, shrugged their shoulders and went back to work.

"Well, get back to work, Johnson, and take it easy. You don't have to impress me. I know what a good worker you are."

That this black man seemed to know his job as well as he seemed to understand the unspoken dynamics of his unique situation must be taken for granted. For were this not so, he would not have been a part of this collection of sinew and muscle, of sweat and concerted manual labor; would not have been with this same gang for many Christmas drinks from bottles cozened in brown paper bags—passed around behind the back of the truck before each went off to separate neighborhoods on the last workday before the holidays. He would not have been the recipient of a collection of ten moist, crumpled one-dollar bills stuffed inside an unsigned card from his fellow workers when his mother died. The most assured sign of his tenure was the fact that they allowed him to ride in the cab with the others as they made their way from one section of the city to another, where he was equally as unwanted, except during daylight hours.

Few words were spoken between them, despite the sheath of days that witnessed their communal efforts. The men simply went about their tasks of fixing the fixable and mouthing expletives over that which was outside their ability to remedy—that day. Despite their familiarity with the labor, despite the mind-numbing sameness of the tasks that lay before them, unconscious of the way their individual strengths and skills had coalesced into one efficient unit, even so, on this day, the sun eventually had taken its toll and the men began to flag.

The owners of the row house directly in front of where they worked had sat inside seeking shelter from the merciless heat. The scorching temperature inside was abetted by the conductive nature of traditional regional flat tar-covered roofs and was exacerbated by the tar-covered roadway and the belching, roiling, stinking tar pot a scant few feet from the front door near where the crew worked. Conditions were made even less tolerable because the ruptured terra cotta sewer line added a noxious element to the deadened air.

The front striped awning of green and white was lowered to restrict the oppressive elements, but it could not keep out the stench of bubbling asphalt or the smell of human waste. The white-corded Venetian blinds were drawn in a futile attempt to cocoon the occupants against the force of the brilliance that carried with it the July heat. But blinds, too, were no real match against the efforts of nature or the failure of human progress.

Now and then, one of the crew noticed that the blinds surrendered their perfectly repeating linear forms and created a V-shaped mouth—a vantage point from which protruded a slender, bony finger. Sometimes, they actually saw the eyes of a woman. The old woman, to whom these appendages belonged, operated like a second foreman. Every fifteen minutes or so, all day long, she freed herself from the tenacious grip of the vinyl slipcovers on her Sears & Roebuck recliner, released the cotton material of her pink and blue housecoat that fastened itself with sweat to her seemingly ancient frame and braved the sweltering heat of the enclosed porch so she could check on the men's progress.

Perhaps she was trying to equate the cost of the job with the volume of sweat that cascaded off the backs of the men, as it stained their shirts and pants. On some jobs, they would have removed their shirts, exposing forms more akin to steel and leather rather than muscle and bone. But because of her presence, they contented themselves with opening their shirts to the waist and pulling the shirttails out of their trousers. Perhaps she had only been bored and sought in their labor some measure of distraction from the heat and from the Sylvania TV that was always on the fritz.

On one of her rare complete appearances, she emerged slowly from the house as if the mere act of walking taxed her to some physical limit. Despite the oppressive heat, she kept the collar of her housecoat closed with a bony hand at her neck. Her blue house shoes made a strange shuffling sound as the unyielding concrete abraded them. She summoned the job boss and asked if the men wanted a cold drink of water. He thanked her profusely, told her not to go to any trouble. Before these banalities forced their way through the rivulets of sweat that formed a small torrent cascading from his red, brush-like mustache, she was gone. In a few minutes, she reappeared with an off-white Tupperware pitcher, which, too, sweated in its attempt to do its job to keep the water cold. She handed him a stack of matching plastic tumblers that were stacked like hats awaiting heads. The foreman handed them out to all the men. They were glad for the respite and even

Theron Wilson Sr., November 24, 1918–December 25, 1994.

more gladdened by the coolness and the restorative power of the water they greedily poured into their parched furnaces. All but one seemed refreshed.

The woman stood and watched them drink as if presiding over an affair of state. She took note of how each man drank, how much he drank, and when he was through, she took his glass and put it back on the tray. She returned once more with refills until almost all were quenched. The men all uttered their thanks and appreciations for her kindness and turned to resume their work. The old woman said nothing as she took the tray and made the same scraping noises back across the concrete, heading for the relative protection of the flat-tarred roof.

When she reached the stairs, before her knurled hand searched out the black wrought-iron handrail, before she opened the white aluminum storm door with its large expanse of glass in the center framed by a grape vine and pineapple motif in plastic, she stopped and put down the tray. The sound of her putting down the tray caught the ears of only Johnson, who turned to watch. Beads of sweat could be seen to form on her wrinkled forehead. He could see the powder she had applied to her face mixed with sweat, forming streaks. The empty tumblers lost their battle with the sun and reflected flatly in the midday haze. And then, she bent over the large galvanized trashcan that sat like a sentinel over the affair by the side of the steps. It was to this sentinel that she commended the glass used by the black man. He alone saw the deft movements of his recent benefactor, movements that escaped the notice of the others. He alone knew.

There was more to his reaction than was apparent to the naked, unpained eye, but the sweat would not betray his tears, would not mark him as abused, would not open him to pity, or worse, from those who did not see, who might not understand. And so he turned at the sound of his name and went back to work, working with such a hollow vengeance that the job boss told him to slow down. His spirit was at once joined with that of the boiling tar beneath the feet of everyone. He suffered in silence—suffered alone.

Almost a Tear

Philadelphia

By Gary R. Hafer

It was the long, hot, sticky summer of 1974, the season directly after the gasoline crisis in the Northeast, the time Goog kept a loaded revolver in his desk "just in case." But I was just a kid, sixteen, and its memory faded as if I were peering down a long, deep tunnel, with me emerging at the other end, unscathed and unaffected and unaware. Besides, I had just gotten up for another Saturday of weekend work that seemed so much more real to me than anything I was getting in high school.

But what did I know? I was a kid looking to make a buck and revel in the cartoon characters that populated the gas station with their exotic stories and curse words I had never heard before and was instructed not to mimic—that whole realm of adult riddle I was privileged to hear as eavesdropper excited me. Yes, I knew I was a kid—some there even called me *Kid*—but once they made the traditional nod to my youth, they never treated me as a kid afterward.

I was soon in my work coveralls, name stitched above the left breast pocket, ready for another day at Goog's Service Station. That was important, Goog said: appropriating "service station" instead of "gas station" in the name because we were selling service. It sounded good anyway, especially when I answered the phone in my official voice. I had worked part-time there since I was thirteen, first waxing cars—the white Riviera driven by Charlie "Broadway" Wagner, the pitching coach of the Boston Red Sox who kept his suburban Philadelphia home—before Goog graduated me with more responsibilities like closing the station on Wednesday nights and Sunday afternoons. Since college was coming up after the next summer, my parents told me to save as much money as I could and work as many hours as possible, which I did, as they had done their entire lives, because they told me to, and, well, I was still that kid standing at the end of the tunnel. I enjoyed working, getting dirty, but mainly, being busy in a city that furnished little enjoyment to a teen with a driver's license and no car.

What I reveled in were Saturdays, always the best day of the week. I could expect to get the most tips and maybe a free lunch from one of the regular clientele who treated the place like a hangout or a barbershop. I *loved* going to work. After some toast with peanut butter and a half cup of instant coffee, I was off, the station keys jumping in my pockets with my quick gait. It was just a one-block walk to the station, past the neighborhood bakery with its hot mix of stale air and baked éclairs. I was happy.

My approach slowed when I reached the main gas pump island. No Louie. That was odd. Louie, the regular mechanic, that cocky, self-confident Missourian, was sure he could do anything. And he could. Louie was everything that I, a dorky high school student, was not: self-assured, a mastermind about cars but especially about girls. He dissected them. What I mean is, he seemed to know their inner workings, not in any deep psychological way but in one that peered inside them, took stock and found what he needed to get what he wanted. It puzzled me why he was dating the boss's daughter, Lois—not that she wasn't stunning with her short brunette hair, which revealed a long neckline. It was excruciating to be near her and sixteen, especially since she seemed genuinely happy to see me whenever she came over to the station to pick up her car. She had a habit of speaking closely, her scent overreaching a sixteen-year-old's sense of wonder. Yet, she didn't seem like a girl who "put out," as Louie called it, but, again, what did I know?

But where was Louie anyway?

The station was silent, waiting for its day. The two massive glass bay doors closed tightly to the asphalt, waiting to be hurled in their tracks upward. The office door with "Lawrence Heffner's AMOCO," perched high above the doorway, a kind of blue-collar translation of a royal passage. I giggled anyway—*Lawrence*. No one called him that, but it baffled me why Goog was any more serious a name.

My laugh fell flat when I faced the glass panes and the locked office door. I fumbled for my set of keys, unlocked the door and placed the stop firmly between the door bottom and the crumbled asphalt tiles. I hurried, too, in rolling out the tire display, filling the metal oil rack with cardboard quarts and unraveling the flags at curbside to proclaim, yes, we were now open.

But open with no Louie. Ah, he was probably just late.

Louie was the kind of guy a high schooler admired. But the admiration was best held at a distance. It was equally as important *not to be* Louie. He was the guy who always had a hot car, in this case a revamped 1958 Chevy Bel Air with sweeping taillights. He used it often to drag race along deserted streets in the early morning when the City's Finest were foiling more devious crimes than his.

"I won," he would declare the same morning at work, his eyes bleary, his body hung over from the night races and the inevitable celebrating afterward. But Louie was the picaresque character one never thought of being. He just was a kind of knickknack on the shelf of figures in one's life. He never knew that, of course. He always thought guys with dull lives like me wanted to be him. But we didn't. In the end, I still don't think he understood that.

I knew the cash drawer bag was hidden in what Goog called the "safe" in the back room—a wooden box without a lock, located in a low shelf, just beside the diesel oil. During Prohibition, Broomy, the former owner, hosted high-stakes card games, feeding players his firewater, hoping the booze would bring betting courage. It never did. Broomy had been a bag man for the mob and a stooge who "ran the numbers" in those days, the whole operation strictly low-class crime. Goog had worked for Broomy before taking over ownership, but the terms of the exchange seemed as murky as Broomy's other business dealings.

After setup, the usual few morning customers trickled to the pumps. Talk was chatty but brief. I wiped a few windshields with a squeegee and read the dipstick with great success. A breeze kicked up, but it simply moved the air without bringing relief: a reason for the flags to flap in the wind. Jim Smith, the carpenter, came in with his truck, looking to pump up his tires before going on a rare Saturday job. The bell on the compressor dutifully rang, announcing each five pounds beautifully and needlessly. Between bell strokes, Jim told me he was going to the Jim Smith Convention next week, a gathering of folks who spared the most popular full-name combination in America. It sounded dull to me, but at least they could ditch the nametags.

I wonder where Louie is.

But soon the landscape changed after I collected the cash from a customer. Goog suddenly appeared around the outside perimeter of the lot in the banged-up Reading Railroad pickup truck he had salvaged from a train yard. The sides were stamped from all the wheel bearings that were dumped from a crane onto the truck bed. The hand-painted lettering with the erroneous "There Goe's Goog" announced more than the painter intended, his work performed for a hot meal and a couple of bucks before wandering off, never to be seen again.

Any vagrant worker was a regular charity for Goog. But there he was now, his smug nose and coal-black hair swept back in lockstep, slamming the truck door shut violently and carrying a tote of coffees and a bag of doughnuts, nodding in my direction before passing into the showroom. All right! Goodies!

Where was Louie?

Yes, something was up. I finished another exact cash sale, and so for the first time since Goog's arrival, I needed to go to the showroom and place the cash in the register. When I did, I saw Goog had positioned himself against the counter that lined all our petroleum products and car-care cosmetics. He made this stance during some high-octane bull sessions, like arguing about Ted Williams's home run record. I knew something big was coming.

"Kid, I'm going to tell you something, and I don't want any questions," he said sternly. I could see circles around his eyes. He hadn't slept. Goog hadn't been in this distemper since he had demanded my Social Security card at sixteen or otherwise I "couldn't work here any more." It was my turn to nod.

"Louie won't be working here any more. I'm going to need your help a couple of nights a week until I find a replacement."

"Of course," I dutifully reported.

Something drained out of me that moment, that curiosity that fueled every Saturday when Louie, in great detail and with precision, laid out his previous night's itinerary. He was "long and lanky," as some of the customers used to refer to him. He was always "working some angle," yet transparently—even innocently—like holding on to his original "Show Me State!" license plate for his '58 Chevy Bel Air.

And that's all Goog ever said to me, but of course, being a kid, I was invisible and found out things anyway. While I was draining the oil in Ed's customized Plymouth four-door sedan—only LDO Super Premium would do—I could hear through the closed showroom door the next bull session erupting as soon as the walk-in trade picked up. *Ding! Ding!* sang the alert cord to tell me a gas customer had just pulled up to the main island. Goog was in his usual bullshitting stance—something he was quite good at—but when I passed the paned windows between the oil bay and showroom, I could hear longer snippets. "She's over home crying her eyes out," he snorted, in a tone sounding supervisory. I still couldn't pull it together.

Hours seem to pass in the same way. The showroom door stayed closed, and the voices drifted out as if they couldn't tolerate the confinement. But the snippets were just that: no connecting thread, variations on a theme I couldn't stitch together.

It wasn't until Louie made an appearance about 11:00 a.m. that I started thinking full time about the big picture. I had a station wagon up on the car rack, pulling tire lugs off and putting them back on with the air hammer, when Louie strolled in in his usual way, cocksure, with that grin on his face as if he had just heard a dirty joke but couldn't tell it to me, not because I was too young, but because he liked having some measure of power over people. It wasn't a mean intention; he just reveled in having any kind of power. He was dressed in a tie and a short-sleeved dress shirt and thin slacks, a wardrobe that draped his frame.

"How's it going, Kid?" he said, slapping me on the arm. The smile widened.

"Okay…good," I said, tentatively.

Goog was right behind me at the tire machine, balancing the tires as soon as I could get them off the station wagon and onto the platform.

"Wait here," Goog said softly and firmly to Louie.

Louie said nothing to Goog or to me. A few moments later, Goog appeared with a white bank envelope and a blank face. Louie took the envelope and slipped it in his breast pocket, unconcerned. "See you around, Kid!" he said, the grin slowly fading as he retreated into the July heat. That was the last time I ever saw him.

In the weeks that followed, I assembled the fragments into a story. While Louie had been taking Lois to the movies and dances and roller-skating in the early evening, he had been taking some other gal to his bed in the later evening. It was only a matter of frequency until he finally got the girl pregnant. And then he decided somewhere along the way that he needed to marry her, and that, of course, affected his whole operation—the later-still night drag racing, the drinking binges with Kempy, the heir-apparent status with Lois's father. The tie and dress shirt were Louie's wedding attire for a ceremony that day before the justice of the peace.

"He could have had the whole place, the whole station and business one day," Goog muttered repeatedly, sometimes to me, but always for himself. I never answered. Even I, as a kid, could see Louie for what he was and not for what he could be. It was simply the triumph of nature over nurture.

———

After Louie left, life at the gas station continued much as it had. I can't remember any customer telling me when Goog wasn't around that he saw Louie across town or at some bar or even pushing a baby carriage.

Everybody pretty much continued in the same quirky manner as before. Of course, there were a few exceptions. Charlie had a pretty long season of minor-league scouting at some remote spots in Pennsylvania and the East, so I didn't see him much that last summer. The last time I saw him was much like the first: his pinstriped suit and signature handkerchief just slightly exposed, the wrinkled face and white hair completing the Broadway image.

But there was a subtle sadness that settled into place. After a while, it was as if it had always been this way, much like those modern questionnaires from health insurance carriers have to be completed with blackened pencil spots in the white bubbles. I'm thinking of one of those statements—"I frequently feel sad"—which makes one think, gosh, I really am sad after all, and didn't I just think the same yesterday? Next, I'm suddenly standing at the end of that dark pipeline again.

A few months later, unexpectedly, Lois got married to someone she met at a dance—it was a quick courtship. "A rebound," Mom said.

The rest of my time at Goog's blurred before my going to college at a West Coast school. It would be a long time before I would see the city again or the parkways where Louie raced under the pale starlight.

I remember asking Goog on that last Saturday if he would miss me. When I think of it now, it was an odd thing for an eighteen-year-old boy to say the week before moving away from the only state in which he had ever lived. Maybe I was hoping that the build-up he had given me for weeks—that he would never be able to replace me—somehow would crest in a final word of praise. But it never did. He said that my leaving would be like a rock thrown into a pond; it produces ripples, registering a sudden impact by its violation. But the ripples would soon spread far and shortly fade. Soon, no one would remember that a rock plunged the depths. No one would ever remember that any ripples had ever appeared in the now quiet pond.

I thought it a strange and hateful thing that Goog would become all metaphorical like that at the end. It was the closest since childhood that I had ever come to shedding a tear.

Author Biographies

TRACY BERTHIN grew up in Ridge Valley, Pennsylvania, and graduated with a BS in English education from Mansfield University in 1995. She then moved to the Finger Lakes region of New York, where she earned her master's in education from SUNY Geneseo and taught high school English and writing in a variety of settings. She currently resides in Avon, New York, with her husband, Dave, and their four children.

DARCY CUMMINGS is a graduate of Penn (literature) and Johns Hopkins (poetry) and is currently studying creative nonfiction at the Rutgers Camden MFA program. She lived, worked and studied in Philadelphia for a large chunk of her life, as well as in New Jersey. Her poetry has appeared in many journals and anthologies in the United States and England; her book, *The Artist as Alice: From a Photographer's Life*, won the Bright Hills Press Competition and was published in 2006. She's received grants and fellowships from the New Jersey State Council on the Arts, the Dodge Foundation, the Virginia Center for the Arts and Yaddo.

MARIA BAIRD GARVIN was born in 1944 and has lived her entire life in Pennsylvania. She has a son, a daughter and three grandchildren. Currently, she resides in the village of Pughtown with her daughter's family.

LAURA M. GIBSON is a former resident of Pennsylvania and a high school teacher. She now writes and lives in the Pacific Northwest, where she teaches elementary school kids about gardening and the virtues of bugs. Her work has appeared in *Passages North*, *Canteen* and the *Sun*, among other journals, and she was recently nominated for a Pushcart Prize. She's currently at work on a novel about a young band of plant thieves who live off the grid.

DEBORAH GOOD was born in Washington, D.C., and grew up surrounded by its color and paradox. In 2003, she moved to Philadelphia, where she is currently a writer and a social researcher. She received her master's in social work in 2009 from Temple University. Her short essays and poetry have appeared in *What Mennonites Are Thinking 2002* (Good Books), *The Other Side* and *Dreamseeker* magazine. She is the author of *Long After I am Gone: A Father-Daughter Memoir* (Cascadia, 2009).

HEATHER E. GOODMAN lives along the Manatawny Creek in Pennsylvania. Her fiction has been published in *Gray's Sporting Journal*, *Whistling Shade*, the *Crab Orchard Review*, *Minnesota Monthly* and the *Chicago Tribune*, where she won the Nelson Algren Award for her story "His Dog."

GARY R. HAFER is the John P. Graham Teaching Professor at Lycoming College in Williamsport, Pennsylvania. His short studies on writing instruction have appeared in *College English*, the *Journal of Developmental Education* and *Computers and Composition*. He is currently finishing two manuscripts, "Write from the Beginning: From My Classroom to Yours," a reflection on pedagogy for professors outside the English discipline, and "Giving Service," a memoir about working at a service station during his adolescence. He is also production design editor for *Brilliant Corners*, a journal of jazz and literature.

CARRIE HAGEN is a writer and researcher who lives in Philadelphia. Overlook Press is publishing *we is got him*, her first book of narrative nonfiction, in August 2011. Her work has won the Christine White Award for Excellence in Literary Journalism and received a nomination for an AWP award. She has an MFA in writing nonfiction from Goucher College.

ADAM HALLER taught English and journalism in Baltimore City for three years and this fall will attend West Virginia University's MFA program. He grew up in Montgomery County, Pennsylvania.

STACEY ZIEGLER HARP was born and raised in Schwenksville, Pennsylvania. She is a magna cum laude graduate of Kutztown University of Pennsylvania.

Stacey left Pennsylvania in 2006 to become a lobbyist in Washington, D.C., but returned home in 2008. Stacey currently lives in Hatboro, Pennsylvania, with her husband, David, and their two rescued pit bulls, Mickey and Tess.

JILLIAN ASHLEY BLAIR IVEY, a native Texan, traded her hometown of El Paso for Philadelphia in 2002 to attend the University of Pennsylvania—and, much to her surprise, she has lived there ever since. Jill has worked in consulting, theater (onstage and off), arts management and marketing and communications, but writing remains her first love. In addition to her current profession, Jill co-edited Phillyist, a website for and about Philadelphians, from 2005 to 2011 and is a founding editor at KeyPulp, an arts and culture web 'zine. Jill is also pursuing her MFA in creative writing at Rutgers University's Camden campus, which is not in Pennsylvania but is within view.

LORI LITCHMAN is a life-long Pennsylvanian who grew up in Northeastern Pennsylvania's coal country. She recently received her MFA in creative nonfiction from Goucher College. When she's not writing, she's usually teaching English to nonnative speakers. She lives in Philadelphia with her husband and their basset hound and tries to find nature anywhere she can in the city.

DIANA MORRIS-BAUER teaches at a high school in Newtown, Pennsylvania. She has her MA in English from Kutztown University. Ms. Morris-Bauer completed a Fulbright teacher exchange year in Germany in 2004–05 and has worked as a translator for the Kloster Indersdorf Holocaust Survivors' Reunion.

BERNARD E.D. WILSON is a native Philadelphian writer who has been published in many venues over the years. He teaches composition and literature at Arcadia University, in Glenside, Pennsylvania. He is also an accomplished musician and somewhat of a car aficionado. Bernard is married and has one son at GWU. He is currently working on his first novel.

About the Editors

REBECCA HELM BEARDSALL teaches in the English Department at DeSales University. She grew up in Quakertown, Pennsylvania, and has lived in various places since 1991, including Scotland, Canada, Montana and, most recently, New Zealand. She graduated with a BA in English from DeSales University in 2005 and received her MA in English from Lehigh University in 2008. She has fifteen years' experience in freelance writing in the United States and abroad. Her poetry has been published in various literary journals. She is co-editor of *Western Pennsylvania Reflections: Stories From the Alleghenies to Lake Erie*. She currently resides in Bellingham, Washington, with her husband and her cat, Myrtle.

COLLEEN LUTZ CLEMENS, a daughter of the Lehigh Valley, is an assistant professor of English at Kutztown University. Along with her poetry publications in *English Journal*, her essay in the anthology *Click* recounts her story of being her high school's first female tuba player. Her essay about her Pappy, who worked at Bethlehem Steel, was featured on Philadelphia public radio's *This I Believe* series. She is co-editor of *Western Pennsylvania Reflections: Stories From the Alleghenies to Lake Erie*. She currently resides in Bucks County with her husband and two dogs.

Visit us at
www.historypress.net